15 ECONOMIC AND PERSONALITY PROFILES— ## <u>ONE OF THEM WILL FIT YOU</u>

- **ON THE WAY UP**—single, college grad, early twenties, income $15,000. Has $5,000 to invest. Willing to assume risk. Goal: the good life.

- **HOUSE RICH**—single-income couple in their late thirties, one teenager, income $60,000. Willing to take only limited risks. Current assets: $100,000 equity in house, plus $20,000. Goals: money for child's education, financial security, minimize taxes.

- **STARTING OVER WITH HELP**—recently divorced, late forties, no dependents, income $12,000. Has a very conservative attitude toward risk. Current assets: $100,000 equity in house, plus $200,000. Goals: financial security, increasing personal earning capacity.

- **EASING INTO RETIREMENT**—dual-earner couple in late fifties with no dependents, income $30,000. Has a very conservative attitude toward risk. Current assets: $75,000 equity in house, plus $50,000 and vested pension rights. Goal: comfortable retirement.

Choose from these or any of the eleven other profiles within and let *New York Times* financial writer Peter Passell teach you how to tailor it—and its corresponding investment strategy—to meet your goals.

*

"A sound introductio

harbors in the widening

D0709157

ALSO BY PETER PASSELL

How To Read The Financial Pages
Where To Put Your Money

PUBLISHED BY
WARNER BOOKS

PERSONALIZED

MONEY

STRATEGIES

15 No-nonsense Investment Plans to Achieve <u>Your</u> Goals

Peter Passell

WARNER BOOKS

A Warner Communications Company

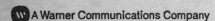

CONTENTS

Introduction   vii

PART ONE: THE CONCEPTS

Too Much Attention to Investments Is Worse
Than Too Little   3

What Worked for Archimedes May Not Work
for You   5

Smart Investors Pay (Some) Taxes   8

Limited Partnerships Can Mean Unlimited Grief   12

Your Broker Is Not Your Friend   15

Neither Is Your Life Insurance Agent   17

Compound Interest Isn't Much Fun at First, but
It Has a Way of Growing on You   20

The Best Investment Is Probably the One You
Live In   23

When in Doubt—Diversify, Diversify, Diversify   25

History Is (Not Quite) Bunk   29

PART TWO: THE TOOLS

Cash—With Interest   39

Fixed Income Investments   55

Investing in Common Stocks   73

Investments with a Tax Edge   96

Precious Metals   123

Hedge Securities   135

Investing for Retirement   143

PART THREE: THE STRATEGIES

On the Way Up   158

And Baby Makes Three   160

v

Ozzie and Harriet, 1980s Style   162
Ambition to Burn   164
House Rich   166
Big Income, Big Responsibilities   168
Business First   170
Hands-on Money Management   172
Refurbishing the Empty Nest   174
Catching Up   176
Starting Over—With Help   178
Easing into Retirement   180
Securing the Good Life   182
Retirement Plus   184
A Well-padded Retirement   186

Afterword   189

Index   193

INTRODUCTION

STAYING AHEAD
OF THE INVESTMENT CROWD

Thinking more about where to put your money—and enjoying it less?

Back in the good old days, when there was just one telephone company and the dollar was worth at least 50 cents, investing seemed so simple. Sure, the mail was full of notes from somebody named James Harrison III (or was it Harrison James III?), promising a free road atlas in return for an evaluation of your insurance and savings needs. Sure, your cousin Freddy said he had this terrific stockbroker who knew this little company that was about to strike oil in a suburb of Des Moines. Sure, the corner bank offered the tough choice of a travel iron or matching his-and-hers manicure sets with every new account.

But sensible folks knew that insurance salespeople bearing gifts should be treated with suspicion, that go-go stocks had a distressing tendency to stop-stop. The place to invest spare cash was in bank savings, maybe utility stocks paying high dividends. Or, to ward off the inflation vampire, a bigger house or a condo at a ski resort.

Today, all bets are off. Other people who bought stocks called Storage Biogenics or MasterTech Peripherals may have been able to trade in their Buicks for BMWs. But when you broke down and bought 200 shares of Storage Bio, it promptly fell from 34 to 6¼. Bank savings certificates paying 11 percent seemed like a great deal—until you heard about tax-free bonds at 12. Even housing, the investment that couldn't go wrong, suddenly looked like it might.

What to do? Television is full of brokers' ads that are long on slogans and short on specifics. One claims a lot of "thank you's" from dowagers climbing out of Rolls-Royces. Another talks and everybody listens. Another makes money the old-fashioned way. Then there's the broker who offers its services to the serious investor—frivolous types need not apply.

Banks are sprucing up their acts, too, inviting customers to invest in everything from variable rate CDs to superNOW accounts to deferred annuities. But half of all their assistant vice-presidents in charge of answering questions seem as bewildered as you are. The other half don't return phone calls.

Well, there are always books . . . and books . . . and more books. Some on their face are unbelievable, promising instant riches the way diet books promise painless weight loss through stuffing your face with seaweed and jamoca almond fudge. Some are inspirational, as if having a positive attitude could help you call the turns in the gold market or choose the better mutual fund.

Still others are three-piece-suit earnest, chock-full of charts showing the Dow Jones averages back to the French Revolution, plus definitions of terms like "American Depository Receipt" and "Butterfly Straddle." But when it comes to practical advice, they are distressingly general. Lower quality corporate bonds are a bit riskier, you may read, but they can be a good buy. A good buy for schoolteachers making $25,000, or for corporate execs pulling down $120,000? Which corporate bonds? Where can you buy them?

Consider what *Personalized Money Strategies* does and does not offer.

- It does not outline a surefire plan for making $2 million in orange juice futures in six short weeks.
- It does not compare the merits of platinum ingots and canned tuna as a hedge against nuclear war.
- It does not even explain what Orson Welles meant by "rosebud."

But:

- *IT DOES TELL YOU WHAT YOU NEED TO KNOW TO STAY AHEAD OF THE INVESTING CROWD, WITH-*

OUT REQUIRING A CRASH COURSE IN COMPUTER PROGRAMMING, SECURITIES LAW, OR THE I CHING.

- *IT DOES TAILOR INVESTMENT STRATEGIES TO YOUR NEEDS—TO HOW MUCH TIME YOU WANT TO SPEND ON MONEY MATTERS, TO HOW MUCH RISK YOU CAN AFFORD TO TAKE WITH YOUR HARD-EARNED DOLLARS. AND IT PROVIDES THE NAMES, ADDRESSES, AND PHONE NUMBERS TO GET THE JOB DONE.*

The first part of this book ("The Concepts") lays out some basics, what's needed to protect yourself against banks, brokers, and other hucksters. The second part ("The Tools") is a no-jargon compilation of how individual investment products work, how they sometimes don't, and where you can buy them. The third part ("The Strategies") matches who you are and what you have to work with to specific investment packages. Not as much fun as seaweed and jamoca almond fudge, perhaps, but you won't be hungry—or broke— an hour later.

Personalized Money Strategies is written to be read straight through with a minimum of head scratching. If you're really in a hurry, though, read "The Concepts" and then go directly to "The Strategies." Pick the ones that come closest to fitting your needs, then refer to "The Tools" for explanations of why specific investments make sense for you.

PART 1
THE CONCEPTS

TOO MUCH ATTENTION TO INVESTMENTS IS WORSE THAN TOO LITTLE

You've heard the horror stories: the skinny guy in accounting who lost $3,000 because he forgot to exercise his stock option; Aunt Mattie, who left $40,000 in expired saving bonds to gather dust in her safe deposit box for a decade; your sister, who was so confused by the breakup of AT&T that she forgot to mail in a change-of-address form for stock dividends.

Investment flubs are often caused by carelessness or a fear of financial matters. For example, about $250 billion now sits in old-fashioned "passbook" savings accounts paying, at best, 5.50 percent. Simply by moving the money to government-insured money market accounts or bank savings certificates, the owners of these deposits earn an extra $10 billion a year in interest.

But for every financial sin of omission, there are probably two sins of commission. In many cases, the losses are small, measurable in wasted time and energy rather than money. Consider, for example, the busy junior executive who devotes her lunch break five or six times a year to switching $5,000 from one bank to another in perpetual quest of the highest interest rate. That might net an extra half percentage point, or $25 a year, in interest. But to earn $25, she will have to spend hours waiting in lines and filling out application forms—not to mention the time spent fighting the bank's computer glitches, or keeping track of the interest earnings for income taxes.

The really serious errors are harder to get a handle on. Your standard, sober-minded guide to the stock market always contains a section on "when to sell"—a few paragraphs about not being afraid to take your losses, a few more about keeping an open mind to new investment ideas. In the abstract, such principles are irrefutable. Trouble is, it's hard to figure that magic moment when it makes sense to sell a stock that has been good to you, or dump the dogs and cats that have kept you awake at night. *As often as not, the decision to trade securities is based on little more than an itch for action*, or a desire to please that nice stockbroker who always remembers to ask about your family.

Ponder the cost of scratching this itch to trade. Commissions on a "round-trip," selling a small amount of, say, General Motors stock and using the proceeds to buy Ford, will cost you 3 to 5 percent of your money. So if you do that twice a year, you are automatically 6 to 10 percent behind. And since relatively conservative investments like General Motors can't be expected to yield, on average, more than 15 to 20 percent a year in dividends and appreciation in share value, that yearning for action may cut your expected income in half.

How much money is actually wasted on pointless securities trades? On a typical day, about 130,000,000 shares of stock change ownership on the national exchanges. If half those trades amount to "churning" (which is what Wall Street calls it), the figure is at least $20 million.

What can you do to avoid churning? Consider first what you shouldn't do.

- *Don't read the stock market pages every day to find out how your 100 shares of Banana Computer are doing.* Sure, you might discover something interesting. But, generally, day-to-day changes reflect nothing significant about the underlying prospects for an investment. For most people, the temptation to treat investing as a respectable form of the daily lottery is too much to resist.

- *Don't do business with a broker who brims with tips about which companies are about to become takeover targets, or which are about to patent a cure for ring-around-the-collar.* Tips are sucker bait. If they were sure things, your broker wouldn't waste his time to earn a few dollars' commission.

- *Don't subscribe to investment newsletters full of authoritative insights on interest rates or gold or the price of June pork bellies.* They're no better than the stockbroker who slipped on Banana Computer.

- *Don't buy securities in expectation of very rapid appreciation.* Some people make money this way. But, then, some people can eat all the french fries they want and never get fat.

If there is a single key here, it's understanding your own weaknesses. If you are simply driven by the need for action, play the market with a small portion of your savings, which you keep in a separate account. Better still, take advantage of mutual funds that allow you to buy and sell at little or no charge. Many groups of mutual funds sold by a single company are tailor-made for would-be churners, offering you the right to switch money by telephone from a growth fund to an income fund to a bond fund to a money market fund for free. See page 90 for a list.

WHAT WORKED FOR ARCHIMEDES MAY NOT WORK FOR YOU

Archimedes, as you probably won't remember from your seventh grade science class, was a mathematician, inventor, defense contractor, and all 'round genius who lived in Sicily 22 centuries ago. When Archimedes wasn't busy measuring the purity of gold ingots in his bathtub ("Eureka, I've found it!") or plotting the destruction of the invading Roman fleet, he thought about lifting things. Heavy things.

According to his principle of leverage, a small force applied over a large distance could be transformed into a large force applied over a short distance. "Give me a place to stand," he is supposed to have said to his buddy, King Hieron, "and I will move the earth."

So much for the science refresher. What does all this have to do with investing? *Just as mechanical leverage permits* small forces to lift rocks, planets, or, for that matter, sticky windows, financial leverage allows small amounts of money to generate large profits.

Say you buy a diamond for $1,000 today and sell it in a year for 20 percent more, or $1,200. That's $200 profit on a $1,000 investment. Not bad, but nothing to slobber over.

Try the deal again, this time with leverage. Buy ten diamonds for $10,000, putting $1,000 down and borrowing the other $9,000 from your rich Uncle Archie. Sell the diamonds after a year for $12,000. Pay back your uncle with, say, $900 interest, and you've got a $1,100 profit. So the same $1,000 invested in the same commodity that appreciated the same 20 percent, generated a $1,100 profit instead of a $200 profit! There must be a catch.

Yes indeed, there must. Make the investment once more, only this time assume that diamonds fall in value by 10 percent instead of rising by 20 percent. Without leverage, you lose $100 of your $1,000. Not good, but no disaster. With leverage, you lose the entire $1,000 investment when you sell off your $10,000 in diamonds for just $9,000. Indeed, counting the interest you owe to Uncle Archie, you end up in debt.

Conclusion: *leveraged investments are a way—one of the few ways—to get rich quick.* Buy any of the dozens of books on how to make a fast zillion in real estate, and you'll find that the "secret" consists of putting down as little as possible on as many properties as possible. *Unfortunately, leveraged investments are also a good way to get poor quick.* If the underlying investment falls in value, even by a little bit, you can lose all your money.

One real uncle, Uncle Sam, takes a dim view of some forms of financial leverage. And with good reason. Back in the 1920s, brokers routinely sold stocks and bonds with as much leverage as possible. Customers would buy, say, $100,000 worth of stock for $10,000 down, using the securities they bought as collateral to borrow the other $90,000. That made the brokers very, very happy because they got commissions for selling more stock. And it made customers very, very happy when stock prices went up.

Trouble is, of course, stock prices didn't always go up. And when they happened to go down one Friday in October 1929, thousands of highly leveraged investors were wiped out. Disaster then fed upon disaster. As stocks began slipping, investors who might otherwise have been willing to wait out the slump were forced to sell in order to make good on their loans. These sales forced other sales in turn, and what might have been only a gray Friday turned decidedly black.

One government reform that followed the Great Crash was a limit on the leverage permitted in publicly traded stocks and bonds. *It's still possible to buy stock on credit, or "margin" as it's known on Wall Street.* Indeed, brokers still push margin sales for the same reasons they pushed them back in the 1920s. *But the Federal Reserve now requires investors to put a minimum of 50 percent down on purchases.*

Uncle Sam is not so demanding on other investments, however. Those who crave leverage can find all the action they want in contracts to buy or sell two dozen different commodities ranging from frozen orange juice to platinum. For example, a typical contract to buy 5,000 bushels of soybeans three months in the future for $6.80 a bushel requires a down payment of only $1,500.

If soybeans then rose from $6.80 a bushel to $7.80 a bushel, you'd clear a $5,000 profit. If, on the other hand, soybeans fell to $6.50, you'd lose every penny of the initial $1,500 stake.

Should you leverage your investments? In a few cases you'd be foolish to pass up the opportunity. Say you routinely finance store purchases on Visa or MasterCard. Credit card finance is always expensive. On the other hand, money borrowed using stock as collateral is relatively cheap, typically 6 or 7 percentage points less than the interest charged on a bank card. So given the choice of borrowing with a credit card (or other unsecured loans) or borrowing the same amount from a broker, by all means, margin your stocks.

More typically, leverage is a matter of judgment. Or rather, personal taste for risk. At one end of the scale are people who simply cannot afford to take chances—investors with modest savings and large responsibilities. At the other end, are people who see investing as just an upscale alternative to slot machines.

There is little in this book about techniques of leverage for two reasons. First, because I am pretty conservative about money and assume my readers are, too. The spectrum of unleveraged securities offers a good choice of "cautiously risky" investments. So for types like us, the only rationale for exercising leverage is to increase our stake where specialized knowledge puts the odds heavily in our favor. Second, because leverage is generally expensive. Markets that offer the most leverage (like the commodities futures market just discussed) usually charge the highest commissions. Anyone for Lotto?

SMART INVESTORS PAY (SOME) TAXES

Mrs. Horace Dodge, the 103-year-old widow of the man they named the car after, had an income of $5 million in 1970. Yet, thanks to the fact that all of it was interest from municipal bonds, she owed not a penny of federal income taxes.

This tidbit was unearthed by Phillip Stern, a journalist and social critic who was making a case for tax reform. But he might also have used it to show that even the very rich can be victims of mediocre investment advice—or, more likely in this case, victims of their loathing for the Internal Revenue Service. *For what really counts to investors with $5 million (or $5,000) is how much is left after taxes. And nine times out of ten, otherwise successful investors who pay no taxes either end up with a smaller spendable income or leave themselves liable for heavy taxes in the future.*

Tax shelters (brokerage houses prefer to call them "tax advantaged investments") come in a variety of shapes, sizes, and flavors. *But all of them—at least all the legal ones— work on one or more of three principles: exemption, credit, or deferral.*

Tax exemption is just what it sounds like. Take Mrs. Dodge's municipal bonds (must I ask twice?). State and local government long ago asserted—and Congress has never challenged—their right to issue bonds whose interest to bondholders was free of federal tax. You don't have to declare such interest on your tax return. If, like Mrs. Dodge, tax-exempt interest is your sole source of income, you don't even have to file a return.

Tax credits are bonuses voted by Congress, meant to reward special interests. Or, as politicians like to say, to encourage socially useful activities. If, for example, you buy a computer for your business (or buy a computer and lease it to someone else's business), you get a credit equal to 10 percent of the purchase price, usable like cash to pay your tax bill.* Congress is particularly fond of tax credits because they are, in effect, a way of handing out money that never shows up on the federal budget as an expenditure. You, too, may love tax credits, provided you have some other good reason to buy a "socially useful" investment like a computer or a solar heating system or, maybe, a windmill.

Tax deferral is trickier to describe because it comes in so many guises. But the underlying idea is pretty simple: by making investments specified in the tax laws, Uncle Sam lets you delay the moment when you must pay taxes on the income generated.

Consider that computer again. Each year, the government lets you deduct an allowance for wear and tear on business equipment from your earnings before figuring the taxes you owe. But the rate at which the computer may be "depreciated" is a legal fiction only vaguely related to (and, typically, much faster than) actual wear. Of course, when you sell the computer or any other capital equipment for more than the law says it's worth, you owe taxes on the difference. So an overly generous depreciation allowance is really only permission to delay the payment of taxes.

Pay now, pay later—big difference? *Big* difference. *At the very least, it's like an interest-free loan from the govern-*

---

*Don't depend on it. As this was being written Congress was considering the abolition of investment tax credits.

ment. And if you haven't been too piggy in using the most generous of Uncle Sam's depreciation formulas, the law gives you an extra bonus in the form of a 60 percent discount on the deferred taxes you finally do pay! More about this and other tax freebees in later chapters.

The standard view about tax shelter is the more the better. *It's true most people earning over $20,000 a year should do some of their saving with investments with tax benefits. But shelter isn't always what it is cracked up to be.*

To begin with, the juiciest tax shelter investments are generally the riskiest. Some of the risk is that you'll be taken by a high-pressure promoter. This is an area in which con artists thrive because many investors are so eager to escape taxes that they lose critical judgment. *But even honest, down-to-earth tax shelters are usually risky because of the nature of the underlying investment.*

Shelters built around real estate are typically leveraged with a lot of borrowed money. That's because the leverage created by a big mortgage allows investors to get the maximum tax-deferral breaks from depreciation. But leverage also implies that the failure to meet income projections— say, because the rental market for office space goes sour— can blow away any possibility of profit.

Other sorts of shelters, such as oil and gas exploration or research and development, may not depend so heavily on risky leverage. But the investment areas themselves are risky. And investors who plunk down 10 or 20 thou must be prepared for the possibility of losing every penny.

Even shelters that perform as promised can generate problems for the unwary. Pick up a copy of the *Wall Street Journal* on any day in November or December (the months investors' thoughts turn to taxes), and you'll notice ads for "3-to-1" or "4-to-1" or even "8-to-1" shelters. The numbers refer to the tax deductions created for each dollar invested. Commit $1,000 to a 3-to-1 shelter and deduct $3,000 from your taxable income over the life of the investment. And so forth.

At first, such shelters seem like magic. If you happen to be in the 50 percent tax bracket, a $1,000 investment in a 3-to-1 shelter gets you $3,000 in deductions. Which reduces your tax liability by half of $3,000, or $1,500. So before your investment ever earns a penny, you are $500 ahead!

Now look again. Uncle Sam isn't quite in the business of giving away free greenbacks. Invariably, most or all of those lovely deductions are based on tax deferral. *At some point, generally four or five years after the initial investment, you will find that the tax shelter turns from a bountiful Dr. Jekyll to a greedy Mr. Hyde,* generating tax liability whether or not the investment is actually producing income. Shelter promoters typically ignore such displeasing details, or simply project enough cash payout from profits or the sale of property to cover the taxes that will eventually be owed. But there's rarely a guarantee that the cash will be forthcoming. And, too often, investors in tax shelters become addicts who must find yet another source of deductions to avoid owing taxes on income spent years ago.

Back to Mrs. Dodge. Her tax shelter—municipal bonds—isn't very risky. Issuers of municipal bonds do occasionally fail to pay. But not often. And since the shelter in municipal bonds comes from tax exemption rather than deferral, Mrs. Dodge was never likely to become a shelter junkie. So what was her problem?

Tax-exempt bonds don't pay as much interest as taxable bonds of equivalent safety and term—which is why they are issued in the first place. They are still a better buy, though, for investors in high tax brackets when you compare after-tax yields. But Mrs. Dodge wasn't in a high tax bracket: she invested her money entirely in tax-exempt municipal bonds. So if she had set aside a few hundred thousand dollars of her millions to invest in, say, taxable U.S. Government bonds, her annual after-tax income would have been several thousand dollars higher. A small price, perhaps, for Mrs. Dodge to pay in order to be able to thumb her nose at Washington. But a few thousand dollars would not be a small price for most of us.

The real point—the overriding point—is that tax shelter is not an end in itself, but a means to an end. *Invest to send the kiddies to Harvard or to buy a house at the beach or to secure a worry-free retirement. Never invest solely to avoid taxes.*

LIMITED PARTNERSHIPS
CAN MEAN UNLIMITED GRIEF

While we're on the topic of tax shelters, consider a related subject—limited partnerships. In theory, they're a great idea. Ordinary business partnerships may work well when it's just you, your brother, and maybe your cousin Freddy. But the arrangements can be cumbersome when dozens or even hundreds of partners are needed to provide cash to operate a business and each of the partners has a different idea about how to operate it.

That's why many investment syndications are set up with two tiers. On top are "general" partners, who organize and control the partnership. Below sit passive "limited" partners, whose only tasks are to contribute capital and (they hope) enjoy the profits.

But it's not only the idea that counts. It's what the people who organize limited partnerships to buy shopping malls, black angus cattle, kung fu movies, fried chicken franchises, and heaven knows what else, do with them. Limited partnerships are now the hottest investment vehicle around, attracting tens of billions of capital from investors in sums as small as $1,000. *Some of them deliver the bacon. More of them deliver only the heartburn.*

With stocks or bonds or mutual funds, brokers charge, at most, 8½ percent in fees to make the investment. With most syndicated investments created around limited partnerships, 8½ percent would be getting off cheap. For example, one super-respectable partnership used to fund the research and development budget of a small drug company paid out commissions totalling 10 percent. *Forbes magazine estimates that fees and commissions in real estate syndications (where minimum investments are usually smaller and selling costs per share higher) average 20 percent.* So, typically, only 80 percent of your money is ever working for you.

The next hurdle, of course, is to figure out what the money will be working on. When you purchase securities listed on one of the major stock exchanges or invest in a publicly traded mutual fund, you have access to a lot of information about what you're buying. Corporations and mutual funds put out annual reports, publish data on past performance, receive ratings from investment services. But when you purchase a $5,000 share in something called Trans-Flo-Co Partners VIII, you're pretty much on your own.

Thanks to the securities laws, Trans-Flo-Co can be sold only to people who read the 168-page prospectus and swear on a stack of old *Wall Street Journals* that they've understood every word of it. But a prospectus is a legal document, written in law school-ese by the sponsor's lawyers to satisfy the requirements of the government's lawyers. *It will list every catastrophe that could conceivably befall partners in Trans-Flo-Co, including the remote possibility that investors may turn into frogs if they kiss the quarterly report. But there will be little, if any, straightforward information about the probabilities of those catastrophes actually happening.* Nor will the 168 pages of charts and figures and dire warnings really offer much insight into the probability of the partnership achieving its profit goals.

Inevitably, then, the real selling is done by salespeople working on commission for the sponsors or for brokerage houses. And unless you happen to be an expert on shopping malls or black angus cattle or kung fu movies, what you end up believing will probably depend more on the verbal skills of the salespeople than on hard facts.

Okay, so you took the plunge. You've become a limited partner in Trans-Flo-Co, and, praise to the gods, it isn't doing badly. But three years have passed, and now you want to sell your shares to make a down payment on the perfect vacation cottage. If Trans-Flo-Co were a stock or a mutual fund, it would be easy to sell. At worst, you'd have to pay a modest commission or accept a depressed price because the stock market was down. But under the Trans-Flo-Co partnership agreement, shares may only be sold with the consent of the general partners. That consent may be readily forthcoming. Then again, it may not.

Ready for more problems? Many (though not all) limited partnerships are tax shelters, investments in which most of the benefits come in the form of tax deductions rather than cash. Now it turns out that Congress can't quite make up its mind about tax shelters. On the one hand, it passes laws that subtly encourage shelter deals. On the other, it frequently expresses horror about all those rich people getting away with fiscal murder and eggs the IRS into interpreting the law to reduce benefits from shelters.

The IRS calls the deals it doesn't like (but may or may not meet the letter of the law) "abusive" tax shelters. Since it can't possibly audit all of the tens of thousands of potentially "abusive" shelters, it uses guerilla warfare to deter their formation. *The latest tactic is a requirement that limited partnerships, which generate substantial tax benefits, be registered in advance with the IRS.* So when you invest in one of them, you must include the registration number on your tax return. That doesn't necessarily mean that you'll be audited. Or, if you are audited, that you'll end up paying extra taxes. But the IRS is serving notice that investors who benefit from tax shelters are their number-one priority.

Does all this mean that syndicated limited partnerships are a bad deal? For most people reading this book, the answer is yes. The risks and the inconvenience will outweigh the potential benefits. In any case, it's hard to make specific recommendations for limited partnerships because too much turns on the details of the specific project. *If you do want to try your hand, though, you can increase the probabilities of success by following a few rules of thumb.*

- *Invest through big brokerage houses or investment companies.* It's not that they necessarily offer the best deals. But if they really mislead you, at least there will be somebody around to sue when the deal goes sour.

- *Spread the risk.* If, say, you want to put $15,000 into partnerships, buy $5,000 shares in three different partnerships, preferably in three different businesses. That will limit your choices because many partnerships require higher minimum investments. And it will mean that you have to put more time and energy into making choices. But it will give you the advantage of diversification, as well as a variety of experience with which to weigh future investment decisions.

- *Be conservative on taxes.* Avoid partnerships that offer more than double the amount you invest in tax deductions. That will eliminate most of the deals that are outright frauds, and it will probably keep the IRS off your back.

- *Buy early in the year.* Sounds silly, but it's true. Lots of investors tend to panic in the late fall and buy anything that promises a big write-off against their current tax liabilities. Early in the year, there is less competition for partnership investments, and correspondingly better deals are available.

YOUR BROKER
IS NOT YOUR FRIEND

Roger W. Wilson, an actor known to teen America as a star of *Porky's* and *Porky's II*, found himself with pots of money and little idea of how to invest it. So in 1981, he placed $2.3 million in an account at a well-known Wall Street brokerage house, giving his broker discretion to buy and sell on his behalf. Two years later, according to Wilson's complaint, all that was left in the account was $1.23.

This case is hardly typical. For one thing, your average millionaire would notice that something was amiss before 99.9999995 percent of his or her principal had been flushed down the drain. For another, very few brokers would "conceal millions of dollars in unauthorized sales and transfers," as Wilson's lawsuits against his brokerage house, broker, lawyer, and accountant allege.

Still, there's a point here for investors with a bit more on the ball than Mr. Wilson and a bit less to invest. *Most brokers are honest, many are charming, some are smart. But, above all, stockbrokers are salespeople working first for themselves and second for you.* They are making a living by buying and selling securities with your money. The more they trade, the more money they make. If you prosper while they prosper, that's fine. If you don't, well . . . everybody has to look out for Numero Uno.

Do you need a "full-service" name-brand broker, the kind that advertises on "Monday Night Football" and charges top-dollar commissions? To begin with, consider what such a broker can't do for you. Those who work for large firms have access to reports from an army of researchers. But *80 percent of the stock-picking research that comes out of Wall Street is repetitive junk.* The hustlers who produce it survive only because clients tend to remember their random successes better than their random failures. You would do as well throwing darts at the stock tables in the *Wall Street Journal*.

The other 20 percent ranges from interesting to downright insightful. However, by the time you hear about it, the brokerage house itself has already made a considerable investment. And chances are, so have thousands of other clients of the firm. Stock recommendations aren't necessarily useless because they are shopworn. If the stock of a large, heavily traded company like IBM or Kodak is a good buy for the first 1,000 people who get the news, it may still be a good buy for the 1,001st. *But too often, the thundering herd has stripped the pasture clean before it's your turn to graze.*

Besides, some recommendations from brokers are guaranteed to be worse than useless. If, for example, you want to buy a mutual fund, your broker will be more than happy to extol the virtues of this growth fund or that income fund. But mutual funds sold by brokerage houses—in contrast to mutual funds bought directly from the fund owners—carry sales charges, or "loads," as high as 8½ percent. *So by purchasing a mutual fund from a full-service broker, you automatically start out as much as 8½ percent behind.*

Now for the good news. Full-service brokers usually have time to chat about the weather and to ask after your kids. More important, they sometimes offer sound advice on general investment and tax questions. Most, for example, wouldn't knowingly peddle a tax-exempt bond to a customer in a very low tax bracket. Most would steer a retiree in need of high current income away from stocks that didn't pay dividends. You can't count on the average broker for sophisticated financial advice. But the majority do know enough to prevent simple errors, or to direct your tough questions to specialists within the firm.

Then there is the convenience factor. *Full-service brokers offer a broader range of investment products than discount brokers or banks.* Some of these products—for example, tax-exempt bond unit trusts—are hard to purchase anywhere else. Most full-service brokerage houses also provide pleasing little extras—for example, monthly statements that can be read without a master's degree in accounting.

Does that add up to sufficient reason to give all your investment business to a full-service broker? Probably not. *The better strategy is to use a discount brokerage service where possible.*

Those who need the basic, unbiased help that brokers sometimes provide can get it for less by purchasing *Money* or *Fact* or *Kiplinger* magazine—or by reading "The Tools" part of this book. Those who want advice in picking specific stocks would do better by reading the interviews with investment advisors in *Barron's*—or by subscribing to a high-quality independent research service, like the Value Line Investment Survey. For help in choosing a discount broker, see page 80.

That still leaves the question of how to choose a full-service broker for specialized investments—tax shelters and the like—that are not available elsewhere. Most of the big brokerage houses sell most of the products at roughly the same commissions. So the primary consideration should be the individual account executive with whom you must deal. And, alas, the only practical way to pick the individual is through referrals from friends or business associates who share your views on investing.

NEITHER IS YOUR LIFE INSURANCE AGENT

You probably know him (or her). He coaches Little League, runs the annual fund-raising drive for the volunteer fire-fighters, and has a nice firm handshake. In fact, he's the salt of the earth in every way but one: much of his livelihood depends on convincing customers to make a bad investment, euphemistically called "permanent" life insurance.

Americans carry nearly $5 trillion worth of life insurance, which works out to about $50,000 for the average family. Some carry much, much more. Too much, in fact. There's rarely a point, after all, in spending a small fortune on insurance so your beneficiaries can live better without you than with you. And some—those without dependents or the prospect of acquiring dependents—probably shouldn't own any at all.

But the idea here is not to calculate how much life insurance is enough. It's to make the distinction between plain life insurance and the curious mixes of insurance and investment so dear to the hearts and wallets of insurance agents.

"Term" life insurance is life insurance. No bells, no whistles; just a bet about how long you will live. You make out a check for the premium. If you don't die, they keep the money. If you do, they pay your beneficiaries the amount specified in the contract. There are variations. With some policies, the premium only goes up every five years; with others, you have the right to increase the size of the policy to keep up with inflation or with growing family responsibilities. But it's easy to comparison-shop because the only really important variable is price.

"Permanent" life insurance—also known as "whole" life insurance, also known as "cash value" life insurance—is a mixture of insurance and investment. You still make out the premium check, but only part of it pays for life insurance. The rest goes into a sort of savings account, with taxes on interest deferred until you withdraw it. Often, the policy calls for a level premium, so you need not worry about shelling out more money as you get older. And at some point, the policy becomes "paid up"—that is, enough cash accumulates in the savings portion to cover the death benefit without further premium payments. At some later date, enough accumulates to start paying out benefits even before you die.

Level premiums . . . tax-deferred savings . . . paid-up benefits . . . cash for retirement . . . Permanent life insurance sounds pretty good, which, presumably is one reason that more than half the people with life insurance opt for it. And in some cases, for some people, it is almost as good as it sounds. But don't hold your breath.

To begin with, insurance companies hardly ever tell you how the total premium is divided between insurance and savings, or what interest rate you get on the accumulated savings. And—surprise!—it usually turns out that the insurance part is very expensive and that the interest rate is very low. A 1979 study by the staff of the Federal Trade Commission (FTC) estimated that the average interest rate paid on insurance savings was just 1.3 percent! *Nobody knows what it is now because, shortly thereafter, the life insurance industry got Congress to pass a law prohibiting further studies.*

Wait, it gets worse. Should you wish to cancel a policy and withdraw the savings, you typically pay big penalties. In cases where you cancel the policy in the first few years, says the FTC, you'll probably get nothing back at all.

In recent years, many consumers have gotten wise to this con game and switched to insurance companies that offer term insurance at rock bottom rates. *Enough consumers, in fact, to scare the traditional life insurance industry into offering more competitive rates.* Today, if you shop long and hard, you may find a permanent policy that pays a decent return on savings and charges relatively light penalties for early withdrawal.

Alternatively, you could try a newfangled product, called "universal" life insurance. Here, you get insurance, plus savings, that pays an explicit interest rate close to the return on long-term corporate bonds. The interest is tax deferred until you withdraw it.

On the other hand, why bother? "Universal" life is no better than the sum of the parts. And since you can always buy term insurance and shelter savings with various tax-deferred investments paying equivalent rates (see page 112), it seems more sensible to shop separately for each.

COMPOUND INTEREST ISN'T MUCH FUN AT FIRST, BUT IT HAS A WAY OF GROWING ON YOU

The ads are guaranteed attention-getters:

- "Deposit $2,000 a year in our E-Z Interest IRA and retire a millionaire."

- "Turn $3,000 into $100,000 in just 30 years—Government Guaranteed!"

- "If you had invested $10,000 in the J. Hart Byrne Maximum Growth Fund in 1955, you would be worth $421,544 today."

The standard response to such pitches is two parts skepticism, one part daydream about what you could buy with $421,544. When some sober consumer-defender type on the "Five O'Clock News" points out that the ads are misleading—that it all has something complicated to do with "compound interest"—daydreams of winters in Palm Springs melt into boredom.

Compound interest is a tad boring. But not nearly so boring as missing out on good investments or, on the other hand, blowing your savings on a sucker deal. So bear with this short lesson on what compound interest can and can't do for you.

Start with noncompounded, or "simple" interest: you deposit $100 at 12 percent interest, and a year later, the bank forks over $112. Suppose, instead, that the bank says it will give you 12 percent, compounded quarterly. What the bank means is that it will figure how much interest it owes you after three months (3 percent of $100, or $3) and add the interest back into your original $100 principal, for a total of $103. After another three months passes, it will figure the interest on $103 ($3.09) and add that back into the principal, for a total of $106.09. Keep this quarterly "compounding" process going for the rest of the year, and you would end up with $112.55, or 55 cents more than you would have received without compounding.

Now start over, assuming the bank pays the 12 percent interest, compounded *monthly*. This time, you would end up with $112.68. Do it once again, compounding *daily*. The total: $112.75.

In this example, the difference in payoff between simple interest and interest compounded daily is just pennies (75 pennies, to be exact). But there are two important ways in which the compounding affects your investments.

First, *frequent compounding allows you to squeeze a bit more interest out of your savings, which means something if the principal is large enough and left in the account long enough.* If Bank A pays 12 percent compounded quarterly, the "effective annual yield"—the equivalent simple interest rate—is 12.55 percent. If bank B pays 12 percent compounded daily, the effective annual yield is 12.75 percent.

How can you figure effective annual yields? You could buy a pocket calculator that includes basic business functions—the Texas Instruments Student Business Analyst-35 is cheap and easy to use. You probably will never have to calculate one yourself, though. *Since the effective annual yield is always higher than the uncompounded interest rate, banks usually go out of their way to provide the information.* If a bank doesn't bother, chances are that's because the bank pays only simple interest on the deposit.

Second, and more important, compounding is the key to those alluring promises of riches, and why they may mislead. Consider that second ad just mentioned, the one guaranteeing to turn $3,000 into $100,000 in just 30 years.* If you were to put $3,000 into an investment paying 12.4 percent annually, you would have a total of $3,372 after the interest payment at the end of the first year. By the end of the second year, you'd have $3,790, and so forth. After the tenth year, the total would be $9,654.

Miracles don't seem to be happening. You're already ten years into the investment, one-third of the way to 30 years. But you are less than one-tenth of the way to $100,000. In fact, the investment is accelerating in value—in the language

---

*The example, by the way, was made up, but is not unrealistic. At the time this is being written, you could buy one form of U.S. treasury bond that would allow you to accumulate even more than $100,000 in 30 years.

of high school math, growing exponentially—as interest on the interest begins to pile up.

In the first year, the interest payment was just $372. In the eleventh year, it will be $1,197. And in the thirtieth year, you would earn $11,009, to reach the $100,000 goal, right on schedule. By the way, if you were to continue this game, plowing back the interest for five more years, you'd have $179,404. Plow it back for a full ten years, and you'd end up with $321,857!*

What's the catch? Why doesn't everybody just buy a slightly cheaper car when they are in their 20's or, maybe, eat out less, and then retire to Palm Springs in the 60's on the earnings from their painless savings?

Actually, there are two catches. The first catch is that we've neglected to account for taxes. If you were in the 30 percent income tax bracket—that is, if you had to pay out 30 cents in taxes for every extra dollar you earned each year in interest—the original $3,000 would only reach $36,000 by the end of the thirtieth year. So *the compounding "miracle" is much more miraculous when it's performed behind a tax shield—say, in a tax-deferred retirement account or in a tax-exempt bond.* More about this in later chapters.

The second catch is the potential impact of inflation. If compound interest can turn today's $3,000 into tomorrow's $100,000, so, too, could compound inflation turn today's $2.95 cheeseburger into tomorrow's $89.95 cheeseburger. Indeed, with 30 years' inflation to account for, $100,000 might conceivably buy less than $3,000 buys today.

But don't let this sobering possibility convince you that there's absolutely no way to win the savings game. No one really knows how much inflation there will be over the next year, let alone the next 30. We do know, though, that periods in which the rate of inflation exceeds interest rates are not common.

Think about it another way. "Real" interest rates—the

---

*Want to figure the effect of compounding without benefit of math tables or a pocket calculator? Try this shorthand trick suggested by economist Burton Malkiel: to find out how long it takes to double your money, divide the interest rate into 72. At 12 percent interest, it takes six years (that's 72 divided by 12. Get it?) At 4 percent interest, it takes about 18 years. And so forth.

nominal rate paid minus the rate of inflation—have generally averaged about 3 percent over the last century. So by targeting a 12 percent return on their money, investors are implicitly betting that inflation will average about 9 percent. *If you invest $2.95 today at 12 percent for 30 years, chances are, you will end up with enough money to buy two cheeseburgers and maybe even a side of fries.*

THE BEST INVESTMENT IS PROBABLY THE ONE YOU LIVE IN

No, this is not a paid message brought to you by your friendly neighborhood building contractor. Yes, it might as well be. *For while home (or apartment) ownership is by no means riskless, for a variety of reasons it is the investment of first choice.* Count the ways.

To begin with, a point so simple that it is often ignored: unlike virtually any other investment, the "income" from the house you live in comes direct, without benefit of middlepersons. To estimate the value of a share of, say, AT&T, you have to guess about all sorts of imponderables— the company's future earnings, how those earnings will translate into the price of a share, how much buying power the dollars will provide, and so forth. By contrast, to estimate the value of the house you plan to live in, all you need to know is how much shelter (and pleasure) it is likely to provide to you.

This special virtue evaporates, of course, when you sell your home. What counts, then, is how much others value your bricks and mortar. And that depends on factors like interest rates, that aren't easy to predict. Still, there is a commonsense argument that *bricks and mortar are a better investment than most of the alternatives.*

Economists say that the value of a security rests with the income it is expected to produce over time. Or, if it produces no income, what the highest bidder will pay for the assets— the buildings, production equipment, factories, mineral resources, and so forth—that it represents. In practice, this can (and does) vary enormously. For example, a factory that makes shoes may lose most of its value simply because a company in Taiwan or Hong Kong starts selling comparable shoes at very low prices.

But people have to live somewhere—and they aren't likely to move to Taiwan because houses are cheaper there. So in all but extreme cases, the value of a house rests on the bedrock of the cost of replacing it with a comparable structure. If you own a pleasant, conventional house in a pleasant neighborhood that would cost $100,000 to duplicate from scratch, the chances are good that, within a period of a few years, someone could be found to pay you at least $100,000 for it. And since construction costs aren't about to fall, this year's $100,000 house could easily become next year's $110,000 house.

Next, *Uncle Sam is apparently so eager for you to invest in your own house or apartment that he doesn't tax the income you derive from it.* Suppose you have a choice of investing $100,000 in a house or $100,000 in AT&T stock and using the income to pay your rent. Buy the stock, and you'll pay income tax on the thousands of dollars in dividends the company mails to you each year. Buy the house, and the government will let you keep the entire "proceeds"—what economists would call the "implicit rent."

Actually, that's only the intangible part of the tax advantage. Say you decide to sell the AT&T shares in order to buy some other stock. You will have to pay income taxes on any appreciation in the value of the shares. However, if you sell the house you live in and buy another for at least as much money within two years, you pay no tax. And if you happen to be over the age of 55, you pay no taxes on realized profits up to $125,000, even if you don't choose to buy another house.

Are these tax breaks fair? Probably not to people who can only afford to invest in a modest house. And certainly not to people who can't afford to own a house at all. But fair or not, Congress isn't likely to change them soon. So if you plan to live in one place for several years and can scratch up the down payment, investment in a house should be a very high priority.

One last thought. This book isn't meant as a manual on house-buying, but I can't resist an opinion about a pressing topic: fixed versus variable rate mortgages. Fixed rate mortgages are the nice old-fashioned kind in which the interest rate and the monthly mortgage payment remain constant for the life of the mortgage. With variable rate mortgages, the interest rate changes periodically to reflect changes in other interest rates in the economy.

Almost all borrowers prefer fixed rate mortgages, and for good reason. If interest rates go up, you're protected. If interest rates fall, you can generally pay off your mortagage with little or no penalty and get a new, cheaper one.

Trouble is, banks prefer variable rate mortgages for an equally good reason. When interest rates rise, they must pay higher rates to depositors in order to stay in business. And to pay those higher rates, they need to link their earnings to fluctuations in interest rates. Banks are so eager to induce borrowers to accept variable rate mortgages that they generally offer them at lower rates—often considerably lower rates.

There is no hard-and-fast rule for deciding whether, say, a 14 percent fixed rate mortgage or a variable rate mortgage starting at, say, 12 percent, is a better deal. But for home-buyers who can afford to take the chance—especially affluent homebuyers who have other investments as well—variable rate mortgages seem to have the edge.

For one thing, interest charges are tax deductible, so Uncle Sam will, in effect, absorb part of the cost of any interest increase. For another, the return on some of your assets (such as money market funds or bank savings certificates) goes up with higher interest rates. So some of your loss as a borrower will be offset by your gain as a lender.

WHEN IN DOUBT—DIVERSIFY, DIVERSIFY, DIVERSIFY

Did John D. Rockefeller, America's first billionaire, make it by investing a little here, a little there? Certainly not. Neither did his modern counterparts, the likes of John Paul Getty (oil), Daniel K. Ludwig (ocean shipping), An Wang (computer hardware), H. L. Hunt (oil), Sam Walton (discount stores), H. Ross Perot (computer services), Forrest E. Mars (candy), David Packard (electronics), and Philip Anschutz (oil).

For that matter, it's pretty tough to amass even $100 million these days without concentrating capital on a single endeavor, then sticking with it long after you have the opportunity to sell for a good profit. So if you sincerely want to become very rich—and are willing to buck the very long odds—skip this section. Better still, skip the rest of the book and wipe the Taster's Choice stains off the dust jacket so you can return it to the bookstore. You'll need the $15.50 more than they do.

For most of us, though, the point of investing isn't to be able to buy Lear jets in matching pastels or to win the America's cup eight years running, but simply to translate personal savings into comfort and security. And to manage that, *no sensible investor will casually put all his or her eggs in one basket*. Actually, there's more to diversification than homilies about eggs and baskets. And it's worthwhile to look a bit harder at the idea.

Heavyweight finance types in business schools think of investments as having (at least) two statistical dimensions: expected return and risk.

Both mean what they sound like they mean. *Expected return* is, on average, the income you think you'll make. If, say, the average return to investors in oil wells were 20 percent, the expected return on an oil well investment you chose at random would be 20 percent.

Not all oil wells, of course, cost the same amount to develop, or produce the same amount of oil. *Risk* is the statistical variation of returns—both higher and lower—around the average. For example, oil wells in proven fields in East Texas are less risky than oil wells in unexplored portions of Alaska because the range of possible results is smaller in the Texas field.

Everybody wants the highest possible expected return for the same reason that practically everyone would rather be rich than poor. But risk is trickier. Some people—for example, all the people who are willing to take big chances to become billionaires—prefer it. In fact, the boom in the new options and futures markets shows that a lot of people are willing to pay high brokerage commissions for the privilege of making investments that resemble casino gambling more than traditional investing. *But more often than not, higher-risk investments must generate a higher expected return in order to attract buyers. And what intelligent diversification does is to give you a way to get those higher expected returns without bearing the higher risk.*

To see what's meant by that, look again at our hypothetical oil field. Let's say that a few particularly well-sited wells will earn a 100 percent annual return, while a few really bad ones will yield nothing but dust. In between are a lot of wells, with an average yield of 20 percent.

Now, give a conservative investor the choice between investing her entire $100,000 savings in a bank deposit paying 10 percent or into just one of the oil wells with an expected return of 20 percent. Chances are, she'd have no choice but to go with the bank deposit. On average, investors in the oil field will earn double the return of investors in the bank deposits. But as attractive as it sounds, a 20 percent return wouldn't be high enough to lure our investor because one of the possible outcomes is no return at all.

Now add a third alternative. Give the conservative investor a chance to put $2,000 into each of 50 wells in the same field. Suddenly, a risky investment in the oil business turns into a virtually riskless investment. The chances of making a killing are gone—a few of the 50 wells may prove to be gushers, but only a few. On the other hand, the chances of losing everything are gone, too. Indeed, if the average well in the entire field generates a 20 percent return, the odds are very good that the return on an investment in 50 randomly chosen wells from the field will be very close to 20 percent.

Sounds great. But how can the diversification principle—lowering risk by spreading your money among many projects whose successes and failures are not linked—be applied in the real world?

Twenty years ago, the answer seemed simple: split your

money between good (translation: high expected return) stocks and good bonds. When the economy was doing well, the stock market would go up along with corporate profits—with, presumably, your well-chosen stocks leading the pack. Bonds, on the other hand, would do relatively poorly during boom times because interest rates would be on the rise. Then, when the economy slowed down, your stocks might sag with it. But any losses would be cushioned by increases in bond values.

The only trouble with the stock/bond strategy is that it doesn't work. *However the theory says they ought to behave, stocks and bonds have gotten into the distressing habit of moving up and down together.* Perfect diversification would require an understanding of all the independent forces that affect the value of securities. Nobody really has a handle on them, in part because it is an immensely difficult problem to analyze, in part because the solution is changing all the time. But two ideas can make a big difference.

First, *mutual funds make sense.* Mutual funds—companies that use your investment dollars to buy many different securities—like to believe they are selling management performance. They buy only good stocks and then sell 'em before they turn sour, or something like that. Some mutual funds do, in fact, beat the market. In general, though, their major virtue is not performance but diversification.

Say you believe that electric utility stocks are a good investment and buy shares in one or two utility companies. You could end up being right in general, but wrong on the specifics: an investment in just a few utility stocks might prove a bust because one of the companies had trouble with a nuclear reactor or was denied an expected rate increase or simply reported lower earnings than had been anticipated. On the other hand, if you bought a mutual fund that invested in 30 or 40 different electric utility stocks, the value of your shares would almost certainly track the general record of the industry.

Second, *stocks aren't enough.* Some mutual funds (and some individual investors) believe they can fashion a portfolio of stocks that can hold its own in any economic climate. Maybe, but there's precious little evidence to support it.

Forbes magazine rates mutual fund performance each year by measuring how well individual funds do in both rising and falling markets. *Of the 340-plus stock funds analyzed in 1984, not a single one that performed in the top eighth during market booms over the previous decade also performed in the top eighth during major market declines.* And only three funds made the top quarter in both categories.

Investors who are serious about diversification must try what, on the surface, seems like a less conservative approach. That means balancing "good times" investments in domestic stocks and bonds with "lean times" investments in precious metals and foreign securities. The most serious investors will also want to consider hedging strategies. More about this on pages 135–143.

HISTORY IS (NOT QUITE) BUNK

Henry Ford, a man almost as adept at producing colorful aphorisms as Model Ts, said it first. Just what Henry had in mind at the time is lost in . . . aah . . . history. But he might as well have been speaking on behalf of the economists and business school honchos who argue that nothing you can learn from studying the past performance of individual stocks (or the stock market as a whole) can help you separate the winning investments from the losers.

Here's how the proponents of this unpleasant theory, known as the "efficient market" hypothesis, argue their case. Some companies, everyone agrees, are better than others. And if you work diligently enough, everyone still agrees, you may be able to spot the ones that will prosper and grow.

Now comes the zinger: so many people are looking so hard at the stock market, argue the efficient-market theorists, that the price of individual stocks always reflects the best available information about the stocks' prospects. While some stocks will undoubtedly do very well over the next year and some will undoubtedly do badly, the probabilities of success and failure are already built into the price of the shares. Research may still tell us which stocks are likely to be volatile and which aren't, giving investors a handle on how much risk they are taking. But as a tool for picking winners and losers, claim the efficient-market theorists, stock research is worthless.

The efficient-market folks go one step further, attacking the separate breed of Wall Street stockpickers known as "chartists." Chartists (as in chart or graph) don't claim to know what the Consolidated Widget Company will earn next quarter. They don't even care what a widget is, or what country Consolidated Widget makes it in. But they do argue that, in the ebb and flow of day-to-day trading, there are consistent patterns relating the number of shares sold and past price changes to future price changes.

Identify those patterns and track them carefully, they say, and you can make a nifty profit betting on the direction of relatively small movements in prices. (Chartism, incidentally, is particularly dear to the hearts of the people who own brokerage houses because chartist advice nearly always requires frequent buying and selling.)

Chartism can't possibly work, counter the efficient-market theorists. Even if there are consistent patterns to be gleaned from the numbers, the very fact that there are so many chartists staring at the same data—and so many investors taking their advice—means that potential money-making opportunities will be impossible to realize. If the charts say "buy," and 10,000 people buy, the bargains thus identified will disappear in a matter of minutes or hours. If the charts say "sell," and 10,000 people attempt to sell, prices will similarly adjust, so there is no money to be made.

Does this mean a whole armada of Wall Street researchers is wasting its time and your money? The efficient-market theory, remember, is only a theory. What counts are results. And, you would think, it would be pretty easy to measure, after the fact, just how well money managers do their jobs.

Actually, it isn't easy, for two reasons. First, it's difficult to separate successes based on luck from successes based on reproducible skill. If 1,000 researchers each offer a list of stocks they say will do better than the averages this year, pure chance guarantees that some of them will be right. This explains why legendarily successful money managers rarely remain legends for very long and why the mutual fund that did so well two years ago probably didn't do well at all last year.

Second, and trickier, is the issue of risk. Volatile stocks, on average, yield a higher return in the long run than stocks with stable, predictable earnings. That's because many investors demand a higher return in exchange for bearing extra risk (see pages 25–29). So merely by confining choices to high-risk stocks, money managers should be able to beat the market averages in the long run. Thus, any acid test of researchers' choices would have to adjust for higher (or lower) than average risk.

As you've probably already guessed, the experts who test the efficient-market hypothesis disagree on the test results. But the best summary of their analyses goes something like this: chartism is almost certainly a waste of time. There isn't any logical basis for the patterns they claim to see. More important, there isn't any evidence that the patterns they do or don't see can help you to beat the market.

On the other hand, recommendations based on the fundamentals of how companies are run, how their share prices compare with those of other companies in the same industry, and so forth, seem to work a bit. That doesn't mean you can rely with confidence on the research-based advice of any broker. But it's comforting to know that what they are trying to do isn't quite impossible.

Now for the punch line. There is one research service— the Value Line Investment Survey—whose stock picks generally beat the market by a healthy margin, even after taking account of risk. Between 1965 and 1983, an investor who once each year adjusted his portfolio of stocks to Value Line's recommendations increased his nest egg 13-fold! More on how to take advantage of Value Line research on page 192.

PART 2
THE TOOLS

THE INVESTMENT MENU AT A GLANCE

	Ease of Access	Minimum Recommended Investment	Expected Return on Investment	Risk of Loss	Tax Advantages	Complexity of Approach	Need for Hands-On Management	Page Reference
Bank Savings Accounts	good	–	low	none	none	easy	none	39
Bank NOW Accounts	best	1,000	low	none	none	easy	none	41
Bank SuperNOW Accounts	best	5,000	med	none	none	easy	none	41
Money Market Funds	best	1,000	med	very low	none	easy	none	43
U.S. Treasury Bills	good	10,000	med	none	some	little	some	43
Short-term Bank CDs	good	500	med	none	none	little	some	44
U.S. Treasury Bonds	good	1,000	high	med	some	little	some	56
Agency Bonds	fair	5,000	high	med	some	little	some	57
Corporate Bonds	fair	5,000	high	med	none	med	some	59
Taxable Bond Unit Trusts	fair	1,000	high	med	none	little	little	62
Taxable Bond Funds	good	1,000	high	med	none	some	little	63
Taxable Zero Coupon Bonds	fair	1,000	high	high	none	some	some	65

	Ease of Access	Minimum Recommended Investment	Expected Return on Investment	Risk of Loss	Tax Advantages	Complexity of Approach	Need for Hands-On Management	Page Reference
Ginnie Maes (GNMAs)	good	20,000	high	med	none	some	some	69
Freddie Mac PCs	good	20,000	high	med	none	some	some	71
Fannie Mae MBSs	good	20,000	high	med	none	some	some	72
CMOs	good	20,000	high	med	none	some	some	72
Ginnie Mae Unit Trusts	good	1,000	high	med	none	little	little	71
Ginnie Mae Funds	good	1,000	high	med	none	little	little	71
Common Stocks	fair	20,000	high	high	some	lots	lots	73
Preferred Stocks	fair	–	high	med	none	lots	lots	79
Growth Mutual Funds	good	1,000	very high	high	some	little	little	86
Balanced Mutual Funds	good	1,000	high	med	some	little	little	87
Income Mutual Funds	good	1,000	high	med	little	little	little	87
Specialized Mutual Funds	good	1,000	high	high	some	some	little	87
Closed-end Mutual Funds	fair	2,000	high	med	little	little	little	93

Long-term Tax-exempt Bonds	poor	10,000	high	med	yes	some	some	96
Prefunded Tax-exempt Bonds	poor	10,000	high	med	yes	some	some	105
Insured Tax-exempt Bonds	fair	10,000	high	med	yes	little	some	101
Zero Coupon Tax-exempt Bonds	poor	5,000	high	high	yes	some	some	105
Tax-exempt Put Bonds	fair	10,000	med	low	yes	some	some	106
Floating Rate Tax-exempt Bonds	poor	10,000	med	low	yes	some	little	106
Tax-exempt Unit Trusts	fair	1,000	high	med	yes	little	little	106
Tax-exempt Bond Funds								
Short term	best	5,000	low	very low	yes	little	little	108
Intermediate term	good	1,000	med	low	yes	little	little	108
Long term	good	1,000	high	med	yes	little	little	108
Deferred Fixed Annuities	fair	5,000	high	very low	some	little	little	112
Deferred Variable Annuities	fair	5,000	high	med	some	some	little	114
U.S. Savings Bonds	fair	25	med	none	some	easy	none	115
Custodial Accounts	poor	1,000	?	?	some	some	little	118
Clifford Trusts	poor	10,000	?	?	some	some	some	118
Gold Bullion	poor	1,000	low	high	some	some	some	125
Gold Certificates	fair	1,000	low	high	some	little	little	128
Gold Mutual Funds	good	1,000	low	high	some	little	little	129
Silver	poor	1,000	low	high	some	some	some	132
Platinum	poor	1,000	low	high	some	some	some	134
Palladium	poor	1,000	low	high	some	some	some	134

CASH—WITH INTEREST

THE MONEY YOU
HAVE TO HAVE FAST

Savvy investors, be they 22 and carefree or 52 and over-whelmed by college tuition bills, keep some of their money in highly liquid form. *Instant access means protection against the unanticipated—a forgotten bill, perhaps, or a really juicy investment opportunity.* And it generally (though not necessarily) means protection against a loss of capital in the face of rapidly changing interest rates.

The big question is *which* liquid investment. Twenty years ago, the answer was easy because the choices were so limited. Most people kept enough cash in an ordinary checking account to keep up with rent, utilities, and credit card charges, then stowed the rest in a savings account. A tiny minority, wiser to the ways of high finance (and with at least $10,000 to spare), purchased U.S. Treasury bills through a bank or broker, or direct by mail from the Federal Reserve.

Today, thanks to the gradual deregulation of the interest rates that banks are permitted to pay, the choices are numerous, and the matter of choosing has become a first-class headache. *But for those who pay even minimal attention, the rewards in terms of convenience and income can be substantial.* Consider the options.

SAVINGS ACCOUNTS

You already know how they work—your grandparents probably opened one in your name with $25 when you were six years old. Day-to-day savings accounts at commercial banks, savings and loans, and credit unions come in the old-fashioned "passbook" variety or the newer "statement savings" versions. For any practical purpose, the two versions are identical. Banks prefer statement savings because the accounts are cheaper to service with computerized bookkeeping equipment.

There is no legal minimum you must keep in a savings account. But banks can, and many do, set their own minimums. Watch out for them: not only can you lose by earning no interest, but you may also pay a penalty of $5 or more a month for the privilege of maintaining the underfunded account. As far as Uncle Sam is concerned, you can withdraw any amount at any time, without penalty. But withdrawals must be made in person or by telephone transfer to another account. You can't write a check on a savings account.

Banks and "thrifts"—the term that lumps together savings and loan associations and their twins, the mutual savings banks—may pay a maximum of 5.5 percent interest from the day of deposit to the day of withdrawal. This interest limit is set to expire in 1986. But you can bet your last peso that banks won't be in a hurry to raise their rates when, and if, the interest ceiling regulation is permitted to expire. Credit unions chartered by the Feds (and most of the ones that are chartered by the states as well) are free to pay any rate on savings accounts. Some do pay a bit more than 5.5 percent to keep their customers from taking their money elsewhere. Savings accounts at federally insured banks, credit unions, and thrifts are protected up to $100,000 per account by one of three quasi-government corporations: the Federal Deposit Insurance Corporation (FDIC), the Federal Savings and Loan Insurance Corporation (FSLIC), the National Credit Union Administration (NCUA).

ORDINARY CHECKING

The just plain vanilla account in a world of mocha chip and heavenly hash. As far as the government's concerned, you may write as many checks as you wish, for any amount (which happens to be on deposit). Checking deposits, like all other deposits in banks that display the FDIC or FSLIC emblems, are insured to $100,000 per account.

Banks can't pay interest on ordinary checking. But they are free to differentiate the product in any other way they like. On the minus side, some banks add a charge for each check or a flat monthly fee for accounts that fall below a specified minimum. On the plus side, some banks give away check forms with pictures of reindeer or George Washington or alpine landscapes. Others offer the convenience of 24-hour computerized tellers or automatic borrowing privileges to cover checks that would otherwise bounce. Still others toss in a Visa or MasterCard with no monthly fees.

NOW ACCOUNTS

Nope, the "now" in NOW accounts isn't an advertising slogan. NOW stands for "negotiated order of withdrawal," which is bank regulator's jargon for a checking account that pays interest. Uncle Sam says that banks and thrifts are welcome to credit interest on NOW accounts at rates up to 5.25 percent, with no minimum balance and no limit on the size or number of checks written. Come April 1986, they will be permitted to pay even higher rates.

If NOW accounts are just checking accounts that pay an interest bonus, why would anyone settle for ordinary checking? Because banks are free to set their own fees and conditions on NOW accounts. *And since few banks wish to function as nonprofit institutions, they generally do set conditions that make ordinary checking a better deal for very small, active accounts.* Some banks charge a flat $5 a month for NOW checking, meaning that you would have to keep about $1,100 on deposit to earn enough interest to break even. Some link monthly charges directly to the average balance kept in the account (the higher the balance, the lower the charge). Some charge for each check written after some maximum is exceeded.

SUPERNOW ACCOUNTS

These are NOW accounts without any government limit on the maximum interest rate paid. The only government requirement (due to self-destruct in 1986) is that you keep a minimum of $1,000 in the account. If the balance in a superNOW falls below $1,000, federal rules limit interest to the regular 5.25 percent rate for NOW accounts.

Same question, different context: why would you ever settle for a NOW account that paid 5.25 percent when you could have a superNOW that paid 7 or 8 percent? Same answer: because banks are one step ahead of you. *Super-NOWs will always pay a few percentage points more than NOWs—month-to-month rates are determined by interest rates in the economy as well as competition for depositors. But virtually all banks impose fees that offset the first $10 or $20 a month in interest earnings.*

Nitpickers note: interest payments on superNOWs, or any other bank account, are taxable as income. But unless the account is maintained for a business, offsetting fees are almost certainly not deductible. So if you earn $325 a year in interest on a superNOW and pay, say, $300 a year in fees, you would have been better off with a checking account with neither interest nor fees.

BANK MONEY MARKET ACCOUNTS

As with superNOW accounts, money market accounts in banks and thrifts are federally insured to $100,000. As with superNOW accounts you must keep at least $1,000 on deposit to earn the posted interest rate. The difference between the two comes down to a trade-off in flexibility versus income.

Federal rules (again, due to be eliminated in 1986) limit the number of checks you can write on a money market account to three a month. On the other hand, *banks always pay higher (unregulated) interest on money market balances than on superNOWs and usually have a friendlier fee schedule as well.*

To gain a competitive edge, by the way, some banks get around the federal check limit on money market accounts by linking them to regular NOW accounts. Say you want to write a $150 check against your money market account. You phone the bank in advance and request that $150 be transferred from your MM account to your NOW. Cumbersome, but perhaps worth the trouble if you value your time less than your money.

MONEY MARKET FUNDS

Cash in a bank money market account is your money, on loan to the bank at specified terms. Cash in a money market fund ceases to be cash at all: it goes to buy shares in a mutual fund, which the managers invest on your behalf.

Does that make much of a difference? Less than you might expect. The money in a money market fund is not guaranteed by a government agency. *But the mutual fund companies that run money market funds are regulated by the Securities and Exchange Commission, and no one has ever lost a penny investing in one.* Unlike banks, money market funds do not guarantee a fixed yield on your money each month. But they invest your money in very secure short-term loans to big banks, companies, and governments, ensuring that the interest rate you do get will be close to the rate paid on other safe "money market" investments.

As with money market accounts, you may withdraw money from a fund (technically, cash in shares) by writing a check or making a phone call. But you're not likely to be able to make a deposit or withdrawal in person because money market funds have no "retail" offices. The mechanics of processing deposits and withdrawals is usually contracted out to a big bank located in some anonymous office building in some anonymous city.

U.S. TREASURY BILLS

A Treasury "bill" (as opposed to a longer-term "note" or "bond") is a loan to the government that Uncle Sam guarantees to repay with interest in one year or less. T-bills are issued in four maturities: 91 days, six months, nine months, one year. *But they are "negotiable"—that is, they may be freely bought and sold after the government issues them.* So it's possible to purchase a T-bill, due to be repaid by the Treasury in any week over the next 52.

Interest rates on T-bills are determined by weekly auctions—the Federal Reserve literally auctions the securities to big institutional investors, such as banks and pension funds, delivering the goods to the bidder who will accept the lowest interest rate. The interest return on 91-day bills typically runs about a half percentage point below the average yield on money market funds. T-bills with longer maturities pay a bit more. The business pages of most big city newspapers include a column on yields for T-bills traded that day.

T-bills are issued in $10,000 minimum denominations, purchasable by individuals direct and without commission from the Federal Reserve or (for a fee) through a bank or stockbroker. They come in "discount" form. You plunk down $10,000. The government immediately returns a small chunk of the $10,000 (perhaps $250 on a 91-day T-bill), which represents a prepayment of the interest you will earn over the short life of the security. Then, when the bill matures, you get a check in the mail (or have the funds delivered electronically to a bank) for the full $10,000. Of course, if you sell a T-bill through a bank or broker in advance of maturity, you'll get less than $10,000. The difference—the "discount"—represents remaining interest owed to maturity, plus brokerage commissions.

Like other interest income, the interest on T-bills is taxed by the IRS. But it is free of state and local tax, which is no small bonus in high-tax states like New York, California, Wisconsin, Massachusetts, and Minnesota.

BANK CERTIFICATES OF DEPOSIT

"Certificate of Deposit," or "CD," is jargon for a savings bond issued by a bank or thrift. Like other deposits at federally insured institutions, they are protected up to $100,000 by the FDIC or the FSLIC. CDs come in terms ranging from 32 days to ten years.

The government imposes no interest floor or ceiling on CDs. Typically, rates paid on very short CDs are about a half percentage point more than the yield on money market accounts. Rates for longer-term CDs typically track rates on government securities. *But if you are in the market for a CD, it's important to shop around. Rates on CDs of any maturity can vary as much as two percentage points from bank to bank and city to city.* Texas and California have been the most competitive regions in recent years.

Until full deregulation (currently scheduled for 1986), issuing banks are obliged to charge a penalty should you withdraw your funds before a certificate matures. The minimum penalty is a month's interest on CDs of a year or less, three months interest on longer terms. Read the fine print, though; those are only the minimum penalties. Banks are free to charge higher penalties if they wish, and some do.

Since all CDs are insured and all require a minimum penalty for premature withdrawal, banks have had to search long and hard for ways to make their CDs look better than the competition's. One device is frequent compounding, which raises the effective annual yield (see pages 20–23). Another is to issue CDs in discount form, like T-bills. You deposit, say, $710, and are guaranteed $1,000 three years later. For information on the advantages and disadvantages, see the section on "zero coupon" bonds on pages 65–68.

Another marketing device is to vary the interest rate paid from month to month, linking payments to yields on T-bills. That saves you the trouble of having to move your money frequently to obtain competitive interest rates. But that virtue is a two-way street: variable rate CDs also spare the bank from having to pay above-market rates, should interest rates fall.

Three more exotic varieties of CDs may catch your eye. "Split-rate" CDs pay a high interest rate to begin with, less later on. *This could prove to be an advantage (rather than just the confusing gimmick it is meant to be) if you wanted to shift taxable income from a high-income year to a low-income year.* In any case, don't be a sucker: be sure to find out what the effective annual yield is over the life of a split-rate CD.

"Expandable" CDs let you add money to an existing CD at the same interest rate, an advantage if interest rates are falling elsewhere. "Convertible-term" CDs start as regular fixed rate, fixed term deposits. But at a specified time a year or two later, you have the option of converting them to variable rate CDs with interest linked to T-bill rates or other bank rates. That's an advantage if rates have risen; useless if they haven't.

MAKING THE CHOICE

Which of these highly liquid investments is right for you? To begin with, consider the one that is wrong for practically everyone—the old-fashioned savings account. Savings accounts are very safe and reasonably convenient, but no more so than other government-insured bank deposits. And they have one huge disadvantage: interest of 5.5 percent or less, far below competitive money market rates. *Savings accounts have been made obsolete by high interest rates. The fact that Americans still keep more than $200 billion in savings accounts can only mean that millions of investors are unaware of the alternatives.*

With savings accounts out of the way, decisions become a bit more difficult. Begin with checking. Almost everyone needs to be able to write several checks each month, so almost everyone needs one of the three types of accounts that permit unlimited checking for sums of any size.

People who keep less than $1,000 in an account will typically do best with ordinary checking. In some cities, though, smaller savings and loans and savings banks use NOW accounts the way supermarkets use weekly specials, giving away NOW services in order to attract customers for other profitable services, such as auto and home improvement loans. Note, however, that free, no-minimum-balance NOW checking is usually no-frill checking—no pretty checkbooks, no shiny gold MasterCards, no 24-hour automated tellers.

People who keep $1,000 to $5,000 will typically do better with NOW accounts than with superNOWs. The interest rate will be lower, but so, typically, will the fees. *If you are one of the unusual high-income individuals who need or want to keep more than $5,000 in checking form, the superNOW may be right for you.* Be sure to shop around, though, comparing services as well as fees and interest rates before making the decision. Remember, too, that the legal distinctions between NOW and superNOW—interest rates and minimum balances—will disappear when all bank interest rates are deregulated, most likely in 1986.

Most investors will want either a bank money market account or a money market fund to supplement ordinary or NOW checking. Frankly, the practical distinctions between the two are small and shrinking. Since most investors will want to keep at least $1,000 on hand, the $1,000 minimum balance requirement on money market accounts is not a significant disadvantage. The more important distinctions are safety and access. Banks are slightly safer because deposits are backed by federal insurance. But the key word here is "slightly": money market funds are very safe, too. And funds do hold a slight edge on access, offering the option of writing more than three checks each month.

Which, then, is right for you? Most likely, the fund or account that pays the highest interest rate or offers the most convenience. When banks were first permitted to promote money market accounts in 1982, most offered higher yields than the funds. Now that the competition has settled down, MM accounts, on average, pay roughly the same rates as MM funds. If you are willing to deal by mail and telephone alone, though, there are always institutions willing to help you beat the average. See the list at the end of this section, page 48.

This leaves T-bills and CDs to consider. T-bills have two advantages. They may be sold (billions worth are, each day) without penalty in advance of maturity. And the interest they generate is free of state and local tax. On the other hand, CDs come in smaller denominations; most banks offer short-term certificates with a minimum size of $500, as opposed to $10,000 for T-bills. CDs, moreover, can be purchased (and rolled over on maturity) without commission, often with a simple phone call. T-bills are easy enough to buy through banks and brokers. But to avoid brokerage fees on the transaction, you do have to do it yourself by mail.

Again, the rational choice probably comes down to convenience and after-tax yield. Shop around, using the yields offered by the banks listed at the end of this chapter to compare with local banks and T-bill rates.

A last consideration. *Because CDs can be cashed in before maturity, it's worth thinking about them as a substitute for money market funds or accounts.* Checkwriting privileges obviously make the MM funds and accounts more convenient to use. However, if you have money you don't expect to need for several months—say, cash set aside for taxes—an extra percentage point or two in interest from a CD could be worth the trouble.

SELECTED MONEY MARKET FUNDS

There are more than 250 money market funds offering similar products. The ones listed here aren't necessarily the best. But all are open to individual investors, and all offer special features that may be of particular interest. Use the toll-free numbers for details on current yield and updates on fund policies. And never invest until you've looked at the prospectus.

Funds investing only in U.S. Government-backed securities.   All funds are safe because all limit investment to banks, companies, and governments that are very unlikely to default on their obligations.

These funds are extra safe because they buy only T-bills and other securities backed by T-bills. Note that the extra safety will cost you a few tenths of a percent in interest.

Capital Preservation Fund
(800) 227-8380—outside California
(800) 982-6150—in California

Dreyfus Money Market Instruments—Government
(800) 645-6561—outside New York City
(718) 895-1206

First Variable Rate Fund for Government Income
(800) 368-2745—outside Maryland
(301) 951-4810

Neuberger and Berman Government Money Fund
(800) 451-2507—outside Massachusetts
(800) 882-2039—in Massachusetts

Rowe Price U.S. Treasury Money Fund
(800) 638-5660—outside Maryland
(301) 547-2308

Scudder Government Money Fund
(800) 225-2470—outside Massachusetts
(617) 482-3990

Vanguard Money Market Trust Federal
(800) 523-7025—outside Pennsylvania
(800) 362-0530—in Pennsylvania

Privately insured fund.   This fund's investments are insured against default by a big insurance company. Not quite as safe as government insurance, but this is splitting hairs.

Vanguard Insured Money Market Portfolio
(800) 523-7025—outside Pennsylvania
(800) 362-0530—in Pennsylvania

Funds with low minimum investment requirements.   Most funds insist on a $1,000 minimum initial deposit. These require only $500.

AARP U.S. Government Money Trust*
(800) 245-4770—outside Pennsylvania
(412) 392-6300

Daily Cash Accumulation
(800) 525-9310

Franklin Group Money Funds
(800) 227-6781—outside California
(800) 632-2180—in California

Funds with low minimums on checking.   Most funds discourage check processing (which costs them 20 to 30 cents a check) by putting a $500 minimum on individual checks. These funds offer increased convenience by allowing checks in smaller denominations.

*Depositors must join the American Association of Retired Persons.

Fidelity Daily Income Trust (no minimum)*
(800) 225-6190—outside Massachusetts
(617) 523-1919

John Hancock Cash Management Trust ($250)
(617) 421-2910

Money Market Management Trust ($250)
(800) 245-2423—outside Pennsylvania
(412) 288-1948

Tax-exempt funds.   These funds buy only short-term tax-exempt securities issued by state and local government authorities. So you don't pay federal taxes on your interest earnings. Remember, though, that the income is subject to state and local taxes, unless otherwise indicated in the prospectus. More important, *consider the fact that the yields on tax-exempt funds are considerably lower than on taxable funds. Unless you have a taxable income of $50,000 or more, you'll be better off with the taxable variety.*

California Tax-Free Money Fund**
(800) 528-6060—outside California
(213) 820-1030

Calvert Tax-Free Reserves Money Market
(800) 368-2748—outside the District of Columbia
(202) 328-4000

Dreyfus Tax-Exempt Money Market Fund
(800) 645-6561—outside New York City
(718) 895-1206

Empire Tax-Free Money Market***
(800) 221-5822—outside New York
(212) 425-6116

---

*There's a catch. The minimum initial deposit is $10,000, and there is a $3 monthly maintenance fee.
**Exempt from California taxes as well.
***Exempt from New York taxes as well.

Lexington Tax-Free Daily Income Fund
(800) 526-4791

Nuveen Tax-Exempt Money Fund
(800) 621-2431—outside New York
(212) 668-9500

Value Line Tax-Exempt Fund—Money Market Portfolio
(800) 223-0818—outside New York
(800) 522-5217—in New York

Vanguard Municipal Bond Fund Money Market Portfolio
(800) 523-7025—outside Pennsylvania
(800) 362-0530—in Pennsylvania

Funds with exchange privileges.   Many money market funds are run by investment companies that also manage a wide variety of mutual funds. To encourage you to invest in their mutual funds, they allow you to switch money market cash into various stock and bond funds at little or no cost. *See the section on mutual funds on pages 84–95 before you take them up on the offer.*

Dreyfus Group Funds
(800) 645-6561—outside New York City
(718) 895-1206

Fidelity Group Money Market Funds
(800) 225-6190—outside Massachusetts
(617) 523-1919

Kemper Money Market Fund
(800) 621-1048—outside Illinois
(312) 346-3223

Rowe Price Group Money Market Funds
(800) 638-5660—outside Maryland
(301) 547-2308

Scudder Group Money Market Funds
(800) 225-2470—outside Massachusetts
(617) 482-3990

SELECTED BANK MONEY MARKET ACCOUNTS

Some people are made so anxious dealing with banks that they simply do business with the first one they find with courteous tellers. Others use the bank that helped them finance homes or cars or businesses or college tuition. Others patronize the corner bank because they believe people in neighborhoods should stick together. However, if your primary concern is the interest you get on money market deposits, it pays to search beyond your own community. *As this is being written, the difference between the highest-yielding money market account and the lowest is over three percentage points!*

These banks are insured by FSLIC or FDIC up to $100,000 per account and provide prompt service by mail and telephone. And they currently have a policy of paying very high rates. Check the ads in the *Wall Street Journal* and the Sunday *New York Times* business section for other banks eager to pay top rates for your cash.

Continental Savings Association
Angleton, Texas
(800) 231-1073

GIT Investment Funds*
Arlington, Virginia
(800) 336-3063

Gill Savings Association
San Antonio, Texas
(800) 531-4455

Pacific Coast Savings and Loan Association
San Francisco, California
(800) 792-7283

Western Gulf Savings and Loan
Bay City, Texas
(800) 457-0005—outside Texas
(800) 392-6619—in Texas

*GIT is a deposit broker, not a bank. It funnels money into insured accounts at a number of banks.

BUYING U.S. TREASURY BILLS

The simplest way is to call up your bank or stockbroker. Most—though not all—will buy or sell T-bills on your behalf for fees averaging $25 per transaction. If you want to save the fee, you can buy T-bills yourself by mailing a certified check to a Federal Reserve district bank. For details on the procedure, write Bureau of Public Debt, Department F, Washington, DC 20226, or telephone the Federal Reserve's information service at (212) 791-5823.

SELECTED BANK CERTIFICATES OF DEPOSIT

Thousands of banks, including the ones near you, issue federally insured CDs. But yields and terms vary enormously. Other things being equal, it certainly pays to shop. *Be sure to compare "effective annual yields" rather than interest rates.* And be careful to check the terms of the CDs, watching out for premature withdrawal penalties that exceed the legal minimum. These banks seem particularly eager for your money; most, though, will pay above-market rates only for deposits over $10,000.

Amalgamated Bank of New York
New York, New York
(212) 255-6200

Beneficial National Bank
Wilmington, Delaware
(800) 441-7084

Butterfield Savings Association
Santa Ana, California
(800) 828-6602

Colonial Savings
Houston, Texas
(713) 784-2260

Crest Savings
Kankakee, Illinois
(800) 842-7378

First Savings and Loan Association
Stockton, Texas
(800) 527-5194

Franklin Savings Association
Ottawa, Kansas
(800) 222-6019

Peoples National Bank of Rockland County
Monsey, New York
(914) 352-9300

Virginia Beach Federal
Virginia Beach, Virginia
(800) 368-3090

Investors who want to find the very highest yields without combing the ads in the financial pages can subscribe to a weekly newsletter called "100 Highest Yields," P.O. Box 402608, Miami Beach, Florida 33408. The newsletter lists effective annual yields for both certificates of deposit and money market funds. A four-week introductory subscription costs $10.

FIXED INCOME INVESTMENTS

IN FOR THE LONG HAUL

Invest in short-term securities like bank savings certificates (CDs) or money market fund shares, and you'll always know that your principal is safe. On the other hand, since interest earnings on these securities fluctuate with market conditions, you'll have only a rough idea of how much income the securities will generate in the future.

Invest in long-term, fixed income securities, like corporate bonds, and you'll know exactly how much interest the bonds will generate for years, maybe even decades, to come. However, *the market value of a fixed income security varies as interest rates in the economy rise and fall.* It's not difficult to see why.

Consider, say, a $1,000 bond issued several years ago by Ma Bell that guarantees to pay the owner $100 a year until the year 2010. If the current yield on bonds recently issued by comparably creditworthy companies—say, General Electric—is 10 percent, the Bell bond will have a resale value of about $1,000. Given the choice, buyers will be virtually indifferent between investing $1,000 to earn 10 percent, or $100 a year, on a newly issued bond from GE, or investing $1,000 to earn $100 on an older bond from AT&T.

Now, suppose interest rates double to 20 percent. Buyers will no longer be willing to pay $1,000 for an old AT&T bond yielding $100 a year because they now could invest the same $1,000 and earn $200 a year on newly issued bonds. So the market price of the AT&T bond must fall to about $500, the price at which the current return on the investment is a comparable 20 percent.

Fixed principal plus fluctuating income, or fixed income plus fluctuating principal: which is the better choice? The answer depends on the needs of the investor and the difference in interest rates paid on long- and short-term securities. If, for example, you are saving for a down payment on a house, preservation of principal is more important than certain knowledge of the amount of interest you'll earn next year. On the other hand, investors who can bear to take the risk might want to invest a substantial portion of their savings in long-term securities that pay two or three percentage points more interest.

For most people at most times, the right choice is compromise, mixing short-term and long-term securities. Here are some of the options available in the long-term category.

U.S. TREASURY BONDS

The U.S. Government issues fixed yield securities with maturities ranging from 91 days to 30 years. Those that mature in five years or more are called Treasury bonds (in contrast to the shorter-term securities called bills and notes).

Treasury bonds come in $1,000 denominations, though the current market price of an older Treasury bond will depend on current interest rates. A bond is identified by its maturity date and initial interest, or "coupon" rate. Thus, a "12 percent Treasury of 1997" will pay $120 a year (actually, $60 every six months) to its owner until 1997, when the face value of $1,000 will be returned.

Newspaper listings for Treasury bonds usually look like this:

RATE	DATE	BID	ASKED	CHG.	YIELD
12½	2009–14 Aug.	101.17	101.20	−.11	12.29

The coupon rate on this bond is 12½ percent, meaning that the Treasury will pay the owner $125 a year, in two payments six months apart. The bond matures in August 2014. When two dates are listed, as in this example, the government reserves the option to pay back the face value to the owners at the earlier date.

The "bid" is the price dealers are willing to pay for the bond, with the digits in front of the decimal referring to the percentage of face value. Just to keep you on your toes, the numbers after the decimal point aren't decimals at all, but 32nds of a percentage point. So a bid of 101.17 translates as 101 and 17/32 percent of $1,000, or $1,015.31. The "asked" column shows the price at which dealers are willing to sell. In this case, it's 1,016.25, or 94 cents more than they would pay for the bond. "Chg." refers to the change in the bid price from the previous day, again in 32nds of a percentage point of face value. Here, the bid price of the bond fell 11/32nds of $10, or $3.44. Got it?

The "Yield" column is the annual interest yield—in this case expressed with honest-to-gosh decimals—that an owner would receive by purchasing the bond for the "asked" price and holding it to maturity in 2014. Note that 12.29 percent is a little less than the 12.50 percent coupon rate. That's because the bond is selling a little bit above face value.

Treasury bonds can be attractive investments for the conservative investor. Government backing makes them free of risk of default (but not the risks associated with interest rate changes). They are highly liquid because billions of dollars worth of Treasury bonds are traded each day. Most stockbrokers and many banks will buy or sell them at very modest commissions. And like other U.S. Government issues, they are free of state and local (but not federal) taxes. This partial tax exemption matters not at all in the few remaining states without an income tax. But it can make quite a difference for high-income investors in high-tax states like New York, California, and Wisconsin.

The price of all this convenience is a lower yield than very safe bonds issued by corporations or by government agencies.

OTHER GOVERNMENT BONDS

The Treasury is the primary issuer of bonds backed by Uncle Sam, but it is by no means the only issuer. So-called "Agency" bonds, bonds from a dozen federal agencies—such as the Federal Land Bank, the Bank for Co-ops, and the Federal

Home Loan Bank—are, in effect, backed by the credit of the U.S. Government. These bonds, listed in major newspapers with the same format and symbols as Treasury bonds, pay a bit more interest—typically a half percentage point.

Why, then, would anybody settle for the lower rates on Treasuries? For one reason only: Agency bonds are less liquid. The difference between the "bid" and "asked" rate is likely to be $5 or $6 on each $1,000 face value bond, rather than $1 to $3 on Treasuries. On the rare occasions when interest rates move sharply, this spread can grow much wider. Liquidity matters a lot to bond speculators and big institutional investors, who may buy and sell $50 million worth of bonds in a day. It should not make much difference to investors who plan to keep the bonds for at least a few years.

The following list covers the relatively popular—and thus relatively liquid—Agency bonds. Stockbrokers and many commercial banks will buy them for you.

AGENCY	MINIMUM PURCHASE
Farmers Home Administration	$25,000
Federal Farm Credit	1,000
Federal Home Loan Banks	10,000
Federal Home Loan Mortgage Corporation	25,000
Federal Housing Administration	1,000
Federal National Mortgage Association	25,000
Small Business Administration	10,000
U.S. Postal Service	5,000

Three international agencies—the World Bank, the Inter-American Development Bank, and the Asian Development Bank—sell bonds to raise money for economic development in the Third World. Investing in Chad or Indonesia may not sound like your cup of tea. *In fact, these bonds are very safe because they are backed by guarantees from governments in North America and Western Europe.* They are, in fact, almost interchangeable with Agency bonds and yield approximately the same interest. Buy them in $1,000 minimums from brokers and some large commercial banks. Remember, though, that unlike Agency bonds, they are not free of state and local tax.

CORPORATE BONDS

Bonds that represent the debt of corporations share many of the features of Treasury bonds. They are issued with a face value of $1,000. They pay interest twice a year. They can be purchased from stockbrokers and specialized bond dealers at relatively low commissions.

But there are big differences, the biggest of which is safety. Some corporate bonds are fully backed, or "collateralized," by specific assets like a fleet of airplanes. If the company fails to pay timely interest, the bondholders' agent has the right to sell the assets to recoup, much the way a bank forecloses on an overdue mortgage. But most corporate bonds are backed solely by the company's own credit.

Before the company can pay dividends to its stockholders, it must pay all the interest and principal due the bondholders. But if it fails to pay, the bondholders' only recourse is to force the company into bankruptcy and wait for the judge to see how much they can get back. That's why the credit ratings, issued by Moody's and Standard and Poor's for individual bond issues, determine what interest rate a company will pay.

A company with the very best credit, like Exxon or IBM, is often able to sell bonds that pay only a percentage point more than Treasury bonds. But reasonably healthy companies that are not in the blue chip league may be forced to pay three or four percentage points more than Uncle Sam. The ratings, incidentally, follow the same scheme as the ratings for tax-exempt bonds. See page 101 for details.

The bonds issued by most large corporations are listed on either the New York Bond Exchange or the much smaller American Bond Exchange. Bonds traded "over the counter"— that is, off an organized exchange—are not necessarily poor credit risks. But they will be less liquid and quite possibly difficult to sell quickly.

Listings of bonds on the two exchanges usually look like this:

BOND	CURRENT YIELD	SALES IN $1,000s	HIGH	LOW	LAST	NET CHG
GMills 8s99	12	3	69	70½	69	−1

This General Mills bond, due to mature in 1999, pays $80 a year in interest on the $1,000 face value. The current yield (as opposed to the yield to maturity listed for Treasury bonds) is simply the interest payment divided by the current price of the bond.

Just three of these bonds were sold this day, at prices ranging from $690 (69 percent of $1,000) to $705 (70½ percent of $1,000). In other words, only about $2,100 worth of these bonds changed hands. That would be a remarkably small dollar volume for a stock listed on an exchange. But it isn't unusual with listed bonds, suggesting just how illiquid corporate bonds can be. Most are held by insurance companies, pension funds, and other institutions that buy them with the intent of keeping them for decades.

Other things being equal, individual purchasers are generally wise to stick with issues that have relatively large markets. These include the bonds of AT&T, the Bell telephone companies, Ford Credit, and GMAC (the car financing subsidiaries for the automakers). If other bonds attract, you can always check the newspaper listings to get an idea of the daily sales volume.

JUNK BONDS: WHAT'S IN A NAME?

For every bond with a gilt-edge rating, there are two issued by companies that can't meet the rating services criteria for high safety. These are casually referred to as "junk bonds."

More often than not, the title is undeserved. To begin with, all long-term bonds (including Treasury bonds) are risky because a change in interest rates will affect their market value. And with all but the most speculative bonds—the obligations of companies near bankruptcy—the risks associated with changes in interest rates are far more significant than the risks of default. As a statistical rule of thumb, the extra interest to be earned on a junk bond is more than enough to compensate investors for taking a chance.

Trouble is, the market for junk bonds is difficult to research, and the bonds are typically illiquid. *The best way to buy junk is through a no-load mutual fund that specializes in them.*

If you want to take the calculated risk, consider one of the following:

American Investors Income Fund
(800) 243-5323—outside Connecticut
(203) 622-1600

Fidelity High Income Fund
(800) 225-6190—outside Massachusetts
(617) 523-1919

Keystone Custodian Funds B-4
(800) 225-2618

Liberty Fund
(212)850-8300

Vanguard High Yield Bond Portfolio
(800) 523-7025—outside Pennsylvania
(800) 362-0530—in Pennsylvania

Like Treasury bonds, the prices of corporates are listed as percentages of face value. Unlike Treasury bonds, there is no decimal, and no confusion about what the numbers after the decimal point mean. The last price paid this particular day for one of the bonds was $690, $10 less than the closing price the previous day.

Treasury bonds cannot be redeemed by the issuer before the maturity date. That's not the case, though, for most corporates. They typically carry a "call" provision in the bond contract, giving the company the option to redeem the bond at a specific price after a specific date. Call provisions work entirely to the issuer's advantage. If the market price of the bond remains below the call price (which is typically $30 or $40 greater than the $1,000 face value), the bond is never redeemed. However, if interest rates fall sharply, the company can call it back at face and borrow the money at a lower cost.

It's important, then, to know exactly what the call provision says before buying a bond. Better still, buy bonds (like the General Mills bond above) that are selling well below face value. That way, if interest rates fall, you, rather than the issuer, will enjoy the windfall as the bond rises in price.

A final thought. In the last few years, corporations have begun to issue bonds with "put" provisions, the buyer's version of a call. They typically give the owner the right to sell bonds back to the issuer at face value after four or five years have elapsed. This put provision doesn't come free: figure you'll get about a percentage point less interest. But the put may well be worth the price since it locks in a floor value for the bond, no matter how high interest rates go.

BOND UNIT TRUSTS

In the world of corporate bonds, it's always a jungle out there. Every bond is a bit different, and every issuer tries to bait a clever trap to induce investors to accept less-than-competitive rates. Therefore, corporate bonds should only be purchased by individuals who have read the prospectus written when the bond was issued. Even then, it pays to diversify by buying bonds issued by several different companies.

Big investors in the market for, say, $100,000 worth of bonds can expect help from a bond broker. But the rest of us who want to buy, say, $5,000 worth are on our own. That's where two different securities created from corporate bonds fit in.

With a corporate bond "unit trust," a major bond dealer

buys several million dollars worth of bonds from a dozen or more companies. The dealer then divides the pile into $1,000 portions, each containing a little bit of each bond issue, and sells the individual portions to the public.

Buyers win in four ways:

1. *For as little as $1,000, the price of one corporate bond, they can diversify into a dozen or more issues.*
2. *Somebody else does the choosing.* They may or may not be the very best bonds in terms of call restrictions or credit ratings. But the dealer is obligated by law to provide a prospectus that clearly outlines the risks.
3. *They are liquid.* Most dealers make a standing offer to buy back the units at their current market value.
4. *They are convenient.* The dealer handles the ongoing paperwork, mailing interest and any repayment of principal to you in a single (typically monthly) check. If you prefer, many will even deposit the monthly cash in your money market fund.

Buyers lose in one way:

1. *The dealer takes a onetime commission of 3 to 4 percent of the purchase price,* considerably more than the commission on the purchase of individual issues. If corporate bonds are right for you, though, this extra fee isn't much to pay for the extra services.

BOND FUNDS

The alternative to a corporate bond unit trust is shares in a mutual fund that buys corporate bonds. The virtues are similar to those of unit trusts. A small amount of cash (sometimes as little as $200) gives you a stake in a lot of different issues. Somebody else does the cooking, as well as the cleaning up: the fund managers choose the bonds and keep track of the cash flow. Typically, the funds give you the option of a quarterly dividend check or automatic reinvestment in fund shares. All funds will buy back your shares at any time for the underlying market value.

Funds claim advantages over unit trusts. As long as you

invest in a "no-load" type of bond fund, there is no charge for buying and no charge for selling. Instead, funds cover costs with annual fees that average about 1 percent. Thus, you could buy and then change your mind three months later without losing a big up-front sales charge. The portfolio in a unit trust is fixed: the same bonds remain in the portfolio until they mature or are called. Funds, on the other hand, trade constantly, with the aim of maximizing income as conditions change. Many, by the way, mix Government bonds with corporates.

In general, then, *bond funds are a better deal for investors who especially value liquidity and believe that fund managers can outguess the market. Unit trusts are better for people who intend to hold on for several years (long enough to compensate for the sales charge) and value the certain knowledge of their monthly income.*

Herewith an abbreviated list of no-load bond funds, with the minimum permissible investment. Note that their investment policies vary from very conservative to moderately swinging. Read the prospectuses before you buy.

D. L. Babson Income Trust ($500)
(800) 821-5591—outside Missouri
(816) 471-5200

Columbia Fixed Income Securities Fund ($1,000)
(800) 547-1037—outside Oregon
(503) 222-3600

Dreyfus A Bond Plus ($2,500)
(800) 645-6561—outside New York
(718) 895-1206

Fidelity Group Bond Funds ($2,500)
(800) 225-6190—outside Massachusetts
(617) 523-1919

Financial Bond Shares ($1,000)
(800) 525-9831—outside Colorado
(303) 779-1233

Liberty Fund ($250)
(212) 850-8300

Rowe Price New Income Fund ($1,000)
(800) 638-5660—outside Maryland
(800) 492-1976—in Maryland

Safeco Special Bond Fund ($200)
(800) 426-6730—outside Washington
(800) 562-6810—in Washington

SteinRoe Bond Fund ($2,500)
(800) 621-0320—outside Illinois
(312) 368-7826

Value Line Bond Fund ($1,000)
(800) 223-0818—outside New York
(212) 687-3965

Vanguard Group Bond Funds ($3,000)
(800) 523-7025—outside Pennsylvania
(800) 362-0530—in Pennsylvania

ZERO COUPON BONDS

If you've been wondering what they'd think of next, wonder no more. "Zero coupon" bonds are securities that accumulate interest until maturity, rather than paying it out twice a year. Zeros are sold at discount from their face value, like U.S. Treasury bills, with the discount reflecting the interest that will be earned on the way to maturity.

Why the fuss? *The big selling point is the chance to invest a pittance. Then, thanks to the miracle of compound interest, come back decades later and collect a small fortune.* One might, for example, buy a zero coupon bond yielding 12 percent due to mature in 20 years. You plunk down $97.22 today. Twenty years from now, you get back $1,000—the $97.22 principal, plus $902.78 interest that has been compounding away at 12 percent all those years. As the table below shows, the longer the time to maturity and the higher the interest rate, the greater the "miracle."

INVEST IN A ZERO COUPON BOND DUE TO MATURE IN THIS MANY YEARS:	IF THE BOND EARNS THIS MUCH INTEREST ANNUALLY:					
	7%	8%	9%	10%	11%	12%
	YOU MUST INVEST THIS MUCH TO END UP WITH $1,000:					
10	$502.57	456.39	414.64	376.89	342.73	311.80
15	$356.28	308.32	267.00	231.38	200.64	174.11
20	$252.57	208.29	171.93	142.05	117.46	97.22
30	$126.93	95.06	71.29	53.54	40.26	30.31

Is the table misleading? No and yes. What you see is what you get—as long, that is, as the company or government issuing the bond is able to meet the whopping financial obligation at maturity. What may mislead, though, is the natural inclination to assume that the $1,000 returned 20 or 30 years later will still be worth $1,000. *Inflation could—indeed, is likely to—reduce the purchasing power of the face value to less spectacular sums (see page 22).*

Still, zeros are more than a marketing gimmick because they offer a certainty of return that no other security can match. Compare a zero to an ordinary bond paying the same 12 percent for the same 20 years. With the ordinary bond, you know you'll get $120 in interest every year. But you won't know what return you'll be able to earn on the $120, should you wish to reinvest it. With a 20-year zero coupon bond, by contrast, you are assured a 12 percent return on accumulated interest, as well as 12 percent on the principal.

This feature makes zero coupon bonds particularly attractive to managers of pension funds and insurance companies, who know they must deliver X dollars a month to Y people 26 years down the road. And it is catching on with individual investors who are accumulating capital for some distant goal like retirement or kids' education, and want to know exactly how much they'll end up with.

Zero coupon bonds come from three sources: corporations, the U.S. Treasury, and state and local governments.

Of the three, *corporate zeros are probably the least attractive to individual investors.* The interest income is, of course, not paid out until maturity. But income taxes are nonetheless due each year on the "implicit" interest. Thus, you end up each year with an extra tax liability and no extra cash to pay it. No less important, corporate zeros often yield surprisingly low rates of interest. In large part, that's because many are targeted to foreign purchasers who enjoy more favorable tax treatment on zeros in their own countries.

As this book is being written, the U.S. Treasury is making up its mind whether to issue zeros. What they decide isn't very important to investors, though, because *Wall Street alchemists long ago figured out how to transform ordinary Treasury bonds into zeros.* A big investment banking house buys a few hundred million dollars worth of T-bonds and strips off the interest coupons entitling the owners to so much money at such-and-such a date. It then stores all the coupons in a vault and issues securities, sold through most stockbrokers, which entitle the buyers to the proceeds.

These "Treasury strips," also known as CATS (Certificates of Accrual on Treasury Securities) or TIGRs (Treasury Investment Growth Receipts), are, in effect, guaranteed by the Treasury. And, unlike many other zero coupon bonds, are fairly liquid. CATS, in fact, are traded on the New York Bond Exchange. Note the disadvantages, however. They usually pay a bit less interest than ordinary Treasury bonds of equivalent term. And owners are liable for federal (though not state or local) taxes on the unpaid, accumulating interest.

State and local governments have also begun to issue zeros. The big advantage is that the accumulating interest isn't taxed by the federal government. Careful, though: states do tax zeros issued by other states. The drawback is that tax-exempt zeros, like any other tax-exempt bond, have lower yields than taxable bonds of equivalent safety and maturity.

Note one other disadvantage—no, call it what it is, a trick. Some tax-exempt zeros are being issued with call provisions that give the issuer the option of buying back the bonds below par. That's just unfair since the whole point of a zero is to be able to lock in yield.

Which zero, if any, is right for you? Forget corporate zeros: you sacrifice too much for too little benefit. Treasury strips are a very conservative investment for IRA or Keogh retirement accounts that are sheltered from taxation (see pages 143–153). They may also be a good investment for Clifford trusts set up by parents to finance their children's college expenses (see page 118). In both cases, the virtues of safety and certainty of return may outweigh the vice of a slightly lower yield to maturity.

Zero coupon tax-exempts offer a convenient form of forced savings to investors who would otherwise be tempted to spend their interest earnings. That can be particularly important in a time of inflation when the principal in an ordinary bond may erode dramatically over 20 or 30 years.

Suppose, for example, you invested $1,000 in an ordinary 30-year bond. If inflation averaged 8 percent a year over the life of the bond, the principal would have the purchasing power of only $99.38 at maturity! One way to protect the principal would be to reinvest the first eight percentage points of interest earned each year, spending only what was left over. The other way would be to invest in a zero coupon bond, in which the interest was automatically reinvested.

But remember: *before you buy a tax-exempt zero, check to make certain there is no call provision.*

PASS THRU SECURITIES

This is another one of those billion dollar ideas so simple you'll wonder why you didn't think of it first.

Say you live in Denver and have $50,000 you would like to invest in some safe, high-interest security. And say there's some nice young couple named Smith-Jones in Orlando, who would be delighted to borrow the $50,000 to buy a house at very attractive terms. The chances that you'll find each other is remote. Even if you did, the chances that you would be willing to part with your money would be small. What do you know, after all, about the value of houses in Orlando? How would you judge the likelihood the Smith-Joneses would make their mortgage payments on time?

That's where the "collateralized pass thru security" fits in. The Smith-Joneses apply to a local bank in Orlando for a mortgage. Provided they (and their house) meet standardized tests of creditworthiness, the bank makes the loan. Then the bank sells the mortgage to one of several federal agencies and private companies that make a secondary market in residential mortgages. The new owner of the mortgage, in turn, packages a big bundle of mortgages with similar maturities and interest terms and resells pieces to pension funds, insurance companies—and private investors in Denver.

Each thin slice, or pass thru security, represents ownership of a fraction of hundreds of different mortgages, usually from dozens of different towns. Each month, the owner of a slice gets a check representing a few dollars from monthly payments on each mortgage. If someone defaults on a mortgage, the owner loses a dollar or two a month until the mortgage is foreclosed and the principal is recovered. Similarly, if someone sells a house and pays off the mortgage prematurely, you get back your share.

Tens of billions of pass thru securities are now sold each year. They have transformed local, and typically inefficient, home mortgage markets into a single national lending forum. Borrowers get loans at minimum cost. Lenders get a higher interest return at lower risk than was previously possible.

What's in it for you as an investor? In a nutshell, a bit more interest than can be earned on bonds of equivalent safety. But not all pass thru securities are alike. Consider some alternatives.

GINNIE MAES (GNMAs)

A federal agency called the Government National Mortgage Association packages federally insured mortgages, adds guarantees of its own, and sells them to investment banks and brokerage houses. The brokers layer on a commission and sell these "Ginnie Maes" to the public in $25,000 minimums. Once a month you get a check for (fully taxable) interest and any return of principal on your specific group of mortgages.

Ginnie Maes have a number of nice features. They are as safe as Treasury bonds yet pay about a percentage point more interest. Ginnie Maes are highly liquid—almost as liquid as Treasury issues. They can be bought or sold through brokers and some commercial banks.

High yield, high security, high liquidity. If this sounds too good to be true, you're right. There are disadvantages.

Since the securities simply pass through interest and principal, you never know how much you'll get each month. Probably more important, you'll never know how long the investment will last. The underlying mortgages have a life of 30 years. But whenever a house is sold or refinanced, the mortgage is liquidated and the principal returned to the owner of the securities. *Owners of Ginnie Maes must keep track of this division lest they inadvertently spend their principal as well as their interest earnings.*

Paradoxically, the most desirable Ginnie Maes to own are those built around mortgages with low interest rates. The yields on such Ginnie Maes are reasonably high because they sell for less than the face value of the security. But there is less chance that the homeowners will pay off their bargain mortgages, allowing you to earn interest longer. And when mortgages are paid off prematurely, you still end up a winner. *You receive a cash windfall representing the difference between the market value of the Ginnie Mae and the face value of the mortgage.* By the same token, the least desirable Ginnie Maes are those based on very high interest mortgages and therefore sell for more than face value.

Confused? Follow this simple rule: no matter how tempting the yield looks, no matter how enthusiastic your broker is, *never buy a Ginnie Mae selling for more than the principal value of the underlying mortgages.*

Newspaper listings for Ginnie Maes, which usually follow the listings for government Agency bonds, look like this:

RATE	BID	ASK	CHG.	YIELD
13	98.26	99.02	−.11	13.07

The mortgages in this pool pay interest of 13 percent on the outstanding balances of the loans. The bid and ask figures are percentages of the face value of the securities, which were initially issued in $25,000 minimums. As with Treasury bonds, the digits to the right of the decimal are 32nds of a percentage point. So if this happens to be a newly minted Ginnie Mae with a face value of $25,000, the price dealers would pay for this would be 98 and 26/32 percent of $25,000, or $24,703.13. The ask price, the price at which dealers would sell the security, is 99 and 2/32 percent of $25,000, or $24,765.63. The change in price since the previous day was 11/32 percent of $25,000, or $85.94. The yield of 13.07 percent (real decimals this time) is the current return on investment, plus the tiny bit of capital gain, as mortgages are refinanced or paid off over an assumed average 12-year life.

Say you want to own Ginnie Maes but don't want to invest anything close to the $25,000 minimum. Consider a "unit trust" consisting of Ginnie Maes rather than bonds (see page 106). They are typically sold in $1,000 minimums through brokers, who maintain a liquid secondary market, should you need to sell. The disadvantage: you pay a 3 to 4 percent commission and thus earn a slightly lower yield on your investment.

The alternative to a unit trust is shares in a mutual fund that invests in Ginnie Maes. Shares, sold in $1,000 minimums, are perfectly liquid since the management of the fund guarantees to buy back shares. And as long as you make sure it's a "no-load" fund, there's no charge for buying or selling.

These funds qualify:

Lexington GNMA Fund
(800) 526-4791—outside New Jersey
(800) 932-0838—in New Jersey

Vanguard GNMA Portfolio
(800) 523-7025—outside Pennsylvania
(800) 362-0530—in Pennsylvania

OTHER MORTGAGE-BACKED SECURITIES

Ginnie Maes are the most popular and most liquid pass thru securities. But they are hardly the only ones around. Another government agency, the Federal Home Loan Mortgage Corporation, issues "Freddie Mac" Participation Certificates (PCs) in $25,000 minimums through brokers. No doubt Freddie Mac's lawyers could list a dozen ways in which they differ from Ginnie Maes. But from the perspective of investors, the only important distinction is that PCs aren't insured by Congress. But the underlying mortgages are insured by private insurance companies, and the pass thru securities are further backed by the considerable net worth of Freddie Mac. *Expect to get about a quarter percentage point more interest in return for the small sacrifice in safety and liquidity.*

The Federal National Mortgage Association (Fannie Mae) is a government-created private corporation. It's pass thru security is called the MBS, short for "mortgage-backed security." MBSs and PCs are close to identical, which is why they pay virtually the same interest rates. Very safe, very liquid. Like other pass-thru's, very attractive to investors in low tax brackets willing to accept the risks associated with changing interest rates.

One last variation on the pass thru security worth noting: the "collateralized mortgage obligation," or CMO. It is meant to appeal to investors who want to reduce the risk that the underlying mortgages will be paid off faster (or slower) than anticipated. Here's how it works.

Freddie Mac, or one of the big private investment banking houses, issues pass thru securities backed by a big pool of mortgages. The securities, called CMOs, are divided into three categories: slow pay, medium pay, fast pay. All owners of CMOs receive monthly checks for interest. But all repayments of principal are directed to the owners of the "fast pay" securities until they are fully paid off. Then all principal goes to "medium pay" security owners. And so forth.

Owners of CMOs don't know exactly when their securities will be redeemed, but they know more than the owners of ordinary pass-thru's. The price of this knowledge—surprise!—is a slightly lower yield.

INVESTING IN COMMON STOCKS

EQUITY—WITH OR WITHOUT SWEAT

In simpler and less cynical times, owning stocks seemed an almost patriotic duty. "Take stock in America" ran the theme of the public service announcements that filled unsold ad space in magazines. There was always a picture of the nicest-looking young family, with a teenage boy and a freckled-faced little girl peering from the windows of their Chevy Impala. Below the image was an inspirational message about hard work and savings and capitalism.

More people own stock than ever before. In 1983, 42 million Americans had some holding of shares or stock mutual funds—double the number in 1965. But these days, owning stock is rarely confused with being a good citizen, and with good reason. Long thought to be a hedge against rising prices, stocks performed miserably during the inflation-ridden 1970s. Still, the stock markets are places where smarts—and luck—can really pay off.

THE BASICS

Common stock is "equity"—ownership rights in an incorporated business. In theory, the owners of the common stock decide how a company will be run and who will run it. They also have claim on the profits after the company's employees, suppliers, creditors, and taxes have been paid.

In practice, small shareholders in large companies have little say in corporate affairs. One hundred shares of General Electric (about .00000022026 percent of the company) will get you a glossy annual report, an invitation to the annual stockholders' meeting, and a voting proxy printed on a computer card. But most shareholders are sufficiently realistic to see their role as passive. When they don't like their company's policies, or when they believe they could make more money elsewhere, they vote by selling the stock.

What are 100 shares of GE stock worth? The short answer—and the only answer many investors think they need—is whatever the next guy will pay for it. But that sort of thinking will make you sucker bait—the prototype small investor whose gullibility for rumors of takeovers and gold strikes and new inventions has paid for more brokers' summer homes than could ever be counted.

There is a good reason for this. *Most "inside information" is nonsense.* Stock prices run up on groundless rumors and then run down just as quickly, leaving the less fleet of phone holding the bag. There is real "inside information" around, but the likelihood you'll hear about it from a friend or a broker before the rest of the world finds out is very small. Think about it: why would some broker let you in on a sure thing for the price of a $200 commission?

Business school types look instead to what they boringly call "the fundamentals," assessing the value of stock the way a farmer would assess the value of a new harvesting machine. A share of GE stock is a claim on the future income of the company. Add up that anticipated profit flow, discounting over time, and you get a number. No one can say for sure how accurate this figure will be, or whether the actual price of the stock will eventually equal its estimated worth. But analysts spend careers making educated guesses, and some of them are right more often than they are wrong.

Two simple measurements offer a shorthand view of a stock. One is the current price divided by the current earnings, known as the PE, or price/earnings ratio. *The more that people are willing to pay for a stock in relation to its current earnings, the faster they expect the company's earnings to grow.* Thus, a company with second-rate management in a declining industry might sell for just three times current earnings. A firm bursting with competence and good ideas might sell for 20 times earnings. The ratio, of course, has no meaning for companies that are losing money.

The other measure is "yield"—the annual cash payout, or dividend, divided by current share price. This looks a lot like the interest on a fixed income security. In industries such as electric utilities that traditionally pay out most of their income to stockholders, it works that way too. *A high yield on a stock, like a high yield on a bond, means that investors think the payout is in jeopardy.* The prices of high-dividend stocks are greatly affected by interest rates in the economy because investors are constantly comparing stock yields to bond yields in search of the best deal.

At the opposite end of the spectrum are companies that pay little or no dividend, no matter how profitable they become. That strategy gives the companies room to build new plants from retained earnings. And it serves the interest of stockholders with large incomes, who would be forced to give the IRS a good portion of their dividend checks. Investors can (or can at least hope to) realize profits by selling shares when they appreciate.

The stock of virtually every company you'd ever hear of used to be listed on either the New York or American stock exchanges. The stocks of smaller companies that couldn't meet the minimum capital requirements—or wouldn't meet the tougher financial disclosure standards—were traded on one of the regional stock exchanges, including the Cincinnati, Philadelphia, Pacific, Midwest, and Boston. Or they were sold the way tax-exempt bonds are still sold, "over the counter," (OTC) through a network of brokers linked by telephone.

A decade ago, it probably did matter where a stock was traded and who did the trading. The volumes of stocks listed on the New York exchange were much higher, so listed securities were more liquid. But regulation, technology, and higher average volumes on all exchanges have changed the securities industry, generally to the advantage of smaller investors. For example, when a stock is listed on more than one exchange, computers now automatically search for the best price. *The OTC market is still less liquid than the big exchanges. But computer matching of buyers and sellers has made it far more efficient than the previous system.*

Brokers still drop hints that only they can ensure a better

"execution"—meaning only they can make certain you don't get stuck with an inferior price as stock prices fluctuate in minute-to-minute trading. Perhaps they once could. Now, it is close to impossible.

HOW NOW DOW-JONES

How's the market doing?

The answer for nine stock watchers in ten is likely to turn on something called the Dow-Jones Industrial Average (DJIA). But this hallowed number, a crudely adjusted sum of the prices of 30 industrial stocks, is hardly a scientifically constructed index of stock prices.

Once upon a time, it came closer. The DJIA represented ownership in a lot of industrial America; when the Dow sneezed, the economy usually caught cold. So powerful was the symbol in fact, that people based psychological theories of stock pricing on its movements: if the Dow breaks through 1000, it will head for 1350 . . . the support levels in a falling market will be around 980 . . .

But the Dow-Jones Industrial Average is no longer a useful tool in following day-to-day market movements because it is neither representative of all traded stocks nor is even weighted according to the size of the individual companies that are represented. Measuring the market by the Dow is like measuring the popularity of the president by sampling the opinions of Lutheran men in their fifties who live in the Midwest. You might manage to concoct some interpretation that made the sample better than picking a number out of a hat. But it wouldn't be easy.

A better candidate for the most representative market index is the New York Stock Exchange Common Stock Index, which covers the 2,300-plus stocks listed on the biggest exchange. Another is the Standard and Poor's 500, an index of 500 large companies, weighted by the number of shares outstanding. Both, though, have a bias toward big. Often, the stock prices of smaller companies will move in the opposite direction.

Truth is, no single index tells you all you might want to know about the stock market. Investors can gain more insight by concentrating on these few, reported in most daily newspapers.

The Standard and Poor's 500—for very large companies

The American Exchange Market Index—for medium-sized companies

The Nasdaq National Market Index—for smaller companies

The New York Stock Exchange specialized stock groups

Industrial index

Transportation index

Utility index

Financial index

Once an order is communicated to the floor of an exchange or an OTC computer, there is no chance you'll be purposely favored (or discriminated against).

Daily listings for the American and New York exchanges and for the National Association of Securities Dealers Automated Quotations (Nasdaq) National Market contain tons of information. Here's what the symbols mean.

52 WEEKS			DIV.	YLD.	PE	SALES				NET
HIGH	LOW	STOCK		%	RATIO	100S	HIGH	LOW	CLOSE	CHG.
28¼	22	DukeP	2.48	8.4	8	2609	u30	29	29½	¾

Before this day, the highest price Duke Power (an electric utility) sold for over the past year was $28.25; the lowest price was $22.00. Most stocks are traded in steps of one-eighth of a dollar. Stocks selling for a few dollars or less may be parsed into 16ths. Duke paid $2.48 per share in dividends over the past year. The yield—that $2.48 dividend divided by the current price—is 8.4 percent. Duke Power's current price is eight times its earnings over the past year. A total of 260,900 shares (2,609 × 100) changed hands this day. A very busy day, indeed, for the company.

The highest price at which the stock traded on this or any other exchange this day was $30. For all we know, though, only a few hundred shares were sold at this price. No seller, in any case, actually received $30 a share because the listing doesn't include brokerage fees or transfer taxes.

The little "u" indicates that $30 was a 52-week high. By the way, a lowercase "d" would indicate a 52-week low. Another dozen lowercase symbols are less frequently to be found wedged into the listing. Consult the box labeled "explanatory notes" at the bottom of the listings page in your newspaper. The lowest price paid for the stock this day was $29. The closing price was $29.50, up by 75 cents from the close the previous day.

Should you buy a stock on your own? By all means, provided you are willing to risk a relatively small amount of your savings to learn more about how the stock market works. Whether you make money or lose money, you will certainly gain some insight into the psychology of risk taking.

If, however, you are a typical individual investor with neither the time nor the money to spare in the name of curiosity, the answer is probably no. Some people do beat the market—since "the market" is an average of many successes and failures, someone has to beat it. A few people even seem to beat the market consistently. But the odds you will join that group are small. So small, in fact, that many professional money managers keep close tabs on "odd lot" transactions, sales and purchases of units of less than 100 shares that are generally attributable to small investors. Then they do the opposite of whatever the odd-lotters seem to be doing.

That cynical strategy, by the way, doesn't work very well, either. If it did, it would suggest that small investors had some collective—if perverse—insight.

NO PREFERENCE FOR PREFERRED

Preferred stock is a hybrid, a cross between "common" stock and corporate bonds. Preferred stock gives you a claim on a fixed dividend, which must be paid before the owners of common stock can receive a single penny. But unlike bondholders, preferred stockholders are not creditors. They cannot demand payment and back up their demand with threats to drive the company into bankruptcy. If a company chooses not to pay a quarterly dividend, that's tough. All preferred dividends past due, must, however, be paid before the common stockholders can get back into the payment line.

As with bonds, most issues of preferred stock contain call provisions. These typically allow the company to buy back the preferred at the issue price any time after five years.

That doesn't sound so great. But it doesn't sound so bad, either. Why, then, do savvy individual investors avoid them? Because preferred stock is so much more valuable to corporate purchasers than to individuals.

Preferred stock can serve as a tax shelter, but only for corporations. They need declare only 15 percent of their income from preferred stock dividends as taxable income. Most profitable corporations are in the 46 percent tax bracket. So a 10 percent yield on preferred stock is the equivalent of a fully taxable 16.4 percent; a 12 percent yield is the fully taxable equivalent of 19.7 percent.

That means that corporations have an incentive to bid up the price of preferred stock to the point where the yields are no higher than the yields on corporate bonds from the same company. From the perspective of individuals, then, preferred stock is the worst of both worlds: more risk than bonds, no chance of dividend growth. If a broker tries to sell

> you some, tell him you want to close your account and are planning to commission a voodoo doll in his image.

If these pessimistic words don't deter you from buying stocks, consider this compromise.

1. Ignore the advice of friends, brokers, and newspaper columnists: what they have to give away or sell is generally useless.
2. Subscribe to the Value Line Investment Survey. Write to 711 Third Avenue, New York, New York 10017, or call (800) 331-1750.

   This is a weekly source of detailed information on 1,700 stocks, with specific buy and sell recommendations. It is more expensive than most competing publications—as of this writing, $37 for ten weeks, $365 for one year. But unlike most competitors, Value Line bases its recommendations on a consistent fundamentalist approach to investing. *More important, with very few exceptions, its choices go up more than the market in good times and go down less in bad times.*
3. Invest at least $20,000 in ten different Value Line–recommended stocks in ten different industry groups. That should be enough to give you the risk-minimizing advantage of diversification. Do not waver on decisions: sell the stocks only if Value Line recommends their sale.
4. Use a discount broker (see below) for all transactions. That will reduce the cost of buying and selling, which can eliminate the profit in an active, otherwise successful investment strategy. Besides, discount brokers give no advice and are thus less likely to deflect you from your path.

CHOOSING A DISCOUNT BROKER

Discount brokers have their drawbacks. They don't sell shares in limited partnership tax shelters. They rarely sell bond unit trusts or deferred annuities or any of a dozen hybrid securities offered by full-service brokers. But they certainly know how to answer the phone, punch up "buy" and "sell" orders on their computer terminals, keep records, and mail out statements. And they do it as well as full-service brokers. *So if you know what you want to buy, it's just plain foolish to spend the money for frills that have no value.*

The decision to use a discount broker still leaves the question of which discount broker. And unfortunately that isn't easy to answer. The actual location of the discounter isn't important. It's no harder or more expensive to dial an "800" number to call across country than it is to phone across town.

The more important issue is the cost of service. Newspaper ads usually list price comparisons with full-service brokers, and in some cases, with other discount brokers. But the numbers can be misleading because no single discounter is cheapest for every conceivable transaction. Some, for example, have lower minimum commissions, offering the best deal for odd-lot sales. Others give extra discounts for high volumes of business. Still others give special discounts for orders placed in off-peak hours, when the stock exchanges are closed.

Mark Coler, a consumer-minded analyst of the discount brokerage business, makes a general distinction between "value" brokers and "share" brokers. Value brokers' charges are more closely linked to the dollar value of the stock being traded. Share brokers, on the other hand, link their charges more closely to the number of shares traded. Thus, if you are buying or selling relatively few shares at a relatively high price—say 100 shares of a $100 stock—the share brokers' commission will be lower. If you are trading a lot of shares at a low price—say 1,000 shares at $10 a share—value brokers will offer you the better deal.

The problem, of course, is that few investors know in advance whether they will be buying a lot of shares of cheap stocks or a few shares of expensive stocks. *One solution is to compromise by dealing with one of the brokers whose price schedule is somewhere between the two extremes. Another, recommended for investors who plan a lot of trading, is to set up two accounts—one at a share broker, one at a volume broker.*

VALUE BROKERS

Marquette de Bary
(800) 221-3305—outside New York
(212) 425-5505

Fidelity Source
(800) 225-2097—outside Massachusetts
(800) 882-1269—in Massachusetts

Charles Schwab
(800) 648-5300—outside California
(800) 792-0988—in California

SHARE BROKERS

Haas Securities
(800) 221-3588—outside New York
(212) 233-1700

Ovest Securities
(800) 221-5713—outside New York
(212) 425-3003

Pace Securities
(800) 221-1660—outside New York
(212) 490-6363

Pacific Brokerage Services
(800) 421-8395—outside California
(800) 421-3214—in California

Wall Street Discount
(800) 221-7990—outside New York
(212) 747-5013

SHARE/VALUE BROKERS

Discount Brokerage
(800) 221-5088—outside New York
(212) 943-8500

Muriel Siebert
(800) 821-8200—outside New York
(212) 248-0600

Parker, Alexander
(800) 221-4872—outside New York
(800) 522-5629—in New York

Quick and Reilly
(800) 221-5220—outside New York
(212) 522-8712

Just to make things more complicated, we offer another alternative. A number of discount brokers have expanded their services to imitate the "asset management" accounts now being promoted by full-service brokers. For a small monthly fee (above any charges for brokerage), these accounts integrate regular brokerage services with one or more money market accounts complete with checkwriting privileges, credit cards, and, in some cases, 24-hour access to funds through automated tellers in banks and airports.

For most people, an asset management account won't do away with the need for regular checking accounts from a local bank. But the combination of discount brokerage with money market and credit card services may prove a real convenience.

If you are interested, check the answers to these questions:

- What is the monthly charge?

- What is the minimum amount of assets—cash and securities combined—required to start the account?

- Is there any minimum sum for which you can write checks?

- Are cancelled checks returned? If not, is there a service charge for photocopies?

- Does the credit card give you access to 24-hour teller machines?

- Is the credit card a true "credit" card, or are charges

deducted from your cash balances as they are pro-
cessed?

* Does the account give you the option of parking your
money in a tax-exempt money market fund?

The four accounts listed below are by no means the only
ones available, but they should give you an idea of the alternatives.

Barclays Asset Management Account
(800) 632-4455—in New York
(516) 482-7500, Extension 375—collect, outside New York

Citibank Focus
(800) 221-2434—outside New York
(800) 522-2188—in New York

Fidelity USA
(800) 544-6666—outside Massachusetts
(617) 523-1919

Schwab One
(800) 227-4444—outside California
(800) 792-0999—in California

COMMON STOCK MUTUAL FUNDS

A mutual fund is really an investment cooperative. Thousands of investors pool their funds, pay managers to make
the investment decisions, then share in the gains or losses.

Funds come in all sizes, shapes, and flavors. Some have
very broad objectives—a mix of current income, capital preservation in lean times, and capital gains in good times
—and seek those goals by investing in a variety of securities.
Others focus on a single industry (health care, gold stocks)
or pursue a specific strategy (hi-tech, small companies,
tracking the stock indexes). Many deliberately take great
risks in search of great profit. Others are rainy day funds,
carefully hedged against capital loss.

The first question is not which mutual funds to buy, but

whether mutual funds are worth buying at all. For most investors in most circumstances, the answer is an emphatic yes. Management fees and, in some cases, sales charges, are a permanent drag on the return to investors. *But sales charges, or "loads" as they are called on Wall Street, can be avoided by buying "no-load" funds direct from their investment company sponsors.* Annual fees, which average a bit more than 1 percent, do reduce income. But they don't look bad when compared with the costs of buying and selling securities on your own.

Now for the really good part. Mutual funds make it possible to invest a small amount of money—sometimes as little as $1,000—in a large number of different securities. *Such diversification offers one of the few truly free lunches available to investors, minimizing the risks in pursuit of maximum gain (see page 25).*

Second, mutual funds increase investors' liquidity. "Open-ended" funds allow you to cash in your holdings for their underlying asset value on a moment's notice. "Closed-end" funds must be sold on an exchange, like ordinary stocks. But their shares are generally more liquid than the portfolio of stocks they own.

Third, mutual funds do the housekeeping. They decide when and where to trade securities. They give you the option of regular cash payments or automatic reinvestment of earnings. They do the paperwork needed for the IRS.

Last, and arguably, least, mutual funds provide professional management. There is a serious debate whether the average mutual fund does better than chance in picking stocks, and whether any mutual fund can hope to beat the averages indefinitely. At minimum, though, *most do what a lot of investors say they would like to do, following consistent investment strategies based on extensive research.*

Load Versus No-Load Funds

Most funds—virtually all common stock funds sold through brokers—have "loads," or sales charges. Typically, the load is 8 percent for purchases under $10,000, declining to 2 or

3 percent for purchases over $100,000. In recent years, some funds have moved to a "low-load" policy, charging 2 to 4 percent up front. Others are "back-end" loaded, charging nothing to buy, but up to 4 percent to sell. A last group might be called "hidden-loaded": there's no charge for buying or selling, but a special surcharge is added to regular management fees for covering advertising and other selling costs.

Mutual fund brokers say that you get what you pay for—that load funds are better managed and make up for the extra charges with extra profits. Some load funds have performed very well, but so have some no-load funds. According to Forbes magazine the averages are virtually a wash: "load" stock funds averaged 17.2 percent annual return over the last decade while no-loads averaged 17.6. It's thus hard to see any reason to pay a sales charge. All the funds analyzed here are no-load.

Fund Objectives

Most funds claim they are somehow special and thus can't be fitted into a few simple categories. Certainly, one should never invest in a fund without reading the management's own explanation of where it plans to go and how it plans to get there. But it's still worthwhile to look at the generalities.

Growth funds seek maximum growth of capital. They usually invest in more volatile stocks that pay little or no dividend. But that need not deter investors who need current income: most growth funds are happy to mail you a fixed monthly check, if necessary liquidating some of your shares in the fund to make the payment. The more serious issue here is risk. Growth funds typically go up more than the market averages in "up" markets, and down more than the averages in "down" markets. Investors who can't stand the heat are best advised to stay out of the kitchen. Or, at least, to invest only a small portion of their assets in risky funds.

Income funds try to maximize current income by investing in high-dividend stocks, sometimes supplemented by bonds or other fixed income securities.   Again, this should not dominate an investor's choice of funds. Investors who don't want to spend current income are welcome to reinvest the dividends. The important distinction is risk. Income funds typically fluctuate in value less than the market as a whole. You are less likely to lose big—or win big—with an income fund.

High-tax-bracket investors should note that income funds invariably generate a lot of taxable income. Growth funds are generally taxed at a lower rate because some of their income is in the form of long-term capital gains.

Balanced funds try to have it both ways—some current income, some potential for capital appreciation.   Investors will end up bearing a medium amount of risk and paying a medium amount of taxes.

Specialized funds are what they sound like.   Some invest only in precious metals, some in foreign stocks, some in small, emerging companies, some in companies doing very poorly that might be on the verge of a turnaround. What they have in common is high risk, which is not necessarily linked to general movements in stock prices. Thus, they make sense for investors interested in very broad diversification.

Rating Mutual Funds

A number of business publications, including *Barron's*, *Business Week*, *Forbes*, and *Fact*, provide periodic scorecards on which mutual funds did best. The value of these numbers is limited, though—funds that made the winner's circle yesterday rarely seem to match the performance tomorrow.

One alternative is to take the long view, picking funds by how well they've done over the last five or ten years. But again, one must make an assumption that more than chance was involved—that the fund managers knew what they were doing right and will continue to do it.

A. J. Liebling, the legendary journalist, once wrote about a con man who understood this subtlety very well. The con man used to pick 36 victims at random—say, dentists from the Chicago Yellow Pages. He would call each one, explaining that he sold tips on horse races. And to prove how good a tipster he was, he would provide a free sample. The con man would then predict the winner of a six-horse race to be run the next day at Belmont, dividing the predictions so that six dentists received the name of each of the horses in the race. The next day, he would call the six dentists who had been randomly given the name of the winning horse, this time offering a second free pick.

Each of the six dentists would again be assigned a horse at random from another six-horse race. And, of course, one dentist would end up with a second winner.

Now comes the sting. The one "winning" dentist, who has no idea there are 35 "losing" dentists, pants for the name of another horse. Our con man obliges—but this time he sells the name for $5,000. If, by chance, the third pick proves to be a winner, he sells a fourth name to the dentist. If not, he starts over with 36 more names—this time, perhaps, accountants in Denver.

Mutual fund managers aren't con men, and there is a very good chance that the funds with the best records over long periods are doing something more than guessing right. So in the short list of funds below, I've included an average annual return figure over the last decade. But that information alone shouldn't be the basis for choosing a fund.

Several other measures are important. One is the inherent riskiness of the fund's investment practices, measured by what business school types call the "beta coefficient." It's complicated to compute, but fairly easy to understand. Beta measures the degree to which a fund is likely to be affected as the stock market moves up or down. A beta of 1.00 means that when the market goes up 20 percent, the value of the mutual fund shares is likely to rise by 20 percent more than it would have risen if the stock market had remained steady. A beta of 2.00 means that the fund would be likely to rise by twice as much as the market—in this example, by 40 percent.

Beta is useful in two ways. First, it tells you how inherently risky your investment is. Very conservative investors, for example, would probably want to avoid funds with very high betas because they are likely to fall sharply when the stock market goes down. Second, it offers some insight into the degree of luck involved in the rise or fall of a mutual fund. A fund with a beta of, say, 1.50, should go up 1.5 times as much as the market simply to hold its own.

What's impressive, then, is a fund that outperforms the market on a risk-adjusted basis. This risk-adjusted annual return is easy to figure: divide the actual return by the fund's beta. For example, a fund with an average annual return of 20 percent and a beta of 2.00, would have a risk-adjusted return of 10 percent. The risk-adjusted return of a fund can then be compared to the return on the Standard and Poor's 500 index (included below)—or to the risk-adjusted return on other funds.

Thanks to the efforts of the American Association of Individual Investors (AAII), betas for mutual funds are now available to the general public. Those figures are reproduced here, along with the risk-adjusted ten-year returns. Readers who would like the most current estimates for fund betas can buy the association's "Individual Investor's Guide to No-Load Mutual Funds," which is updated each August. Send $20 to the AAII, 612 N. Michigan Avenue, Suite 317, Chicago, Illinois 60611, or call (312) 280-0170.

Another way to measure risk is to see how well funds have performed in "down" markets. I've rated the funds below as "above average," "average," or "below average," according to how well they've performed the last three times the market has fallen significantly.

I've included a measure of diversification, based on the calculations of the American Association of Individual Investors. "High" means a fund's good and bad fortunes track the stock market fairly closely. "Low" means a fund tends to go its own way, probably because it invests in a narrow range of stocks. *There probably isn't much point in owning several different mutual funds that are all highly diversified because they will all probably move up and down together.* On the other hand, putting some portion of your assets in a fund that doesn't closely track the stock market could save you some grief when the stock market falls.

Last but not least, I've listed the management expenses of the funds, as a percentage of the value of fund shares for the latest year available. High management expenses don't necessarily make a fund a bad investment. But they are a permanent drag on a fund's net profits and are well worth noting.

Selected Common Stock Mutual Funds

This limited sampling of growth, balanced, and income-oriented funds have all performed relatively well on a risk-adjusted basis. *Don't assume, though, that these funds will continue to perform well, or that funds not included here are necessarily inferior.* A group of specialized funds—some of which have done well, some of which haven't—is also included. A list of funds specializing in precious metals can be found on page 130.

GROWTH FUNDS

NAME/MIN. INVESTMENT	AV. ANN. RETURN	BETA	RISK-ADJ. RETURN	PERF. IN "DOWN" MKT.	DIVERS.	EXP. %
Loomis-Sayles Capital Dev. $250 (800) 223-7124	31.5	1.21	26.0	good	hi	.76
Mutual Shares $1,000 (212) 908-4047	25.4	.63	40.3	good	hi	.83
20th Century Growth no. min. (816) 531-5575	31.3	1.33	23.5	poor	hi	1.02
Tudor $250 (800) 223-3332	22.0	1.21	18.2	good	hi	1.01

NAME/MIN. INVESTMENT	AV. ANN. RETURN	BETA	RISK-ADJ. RETURN	PERF. IN "DOWN" MKT.	DIVERS.	EXP. %
Value Line Leveraged Growth $250 (800) 223-0818	26.7	.77	34.7	good	lo	.80

BALANCED FUNDS

Guardian Mutual $200 (800) 367-0770	19.8	.93	21.3	fair	hi	.67
Ivy Growth $500 (617) 749-1416	17.1	.94	18.2	fair	hi	1.22
Janus $1,000 (800) 225-2618	19.7	.89	22.1	good	lo	1.07
Nicholas $500 (414) 272-6133	25.7	.90	28.6	good	hi	.87
Partners $250 (212) 850-8300	20.0	.58	34.5	good	hi	.97
Windsor $1,500 (800) 523-7025	22.8	.85	26.8	good	hi	.67

INCOME FUNDS

Fidelity Puritan $1,000 (800) 225-6190	17.3	.69	25.1	good	hi	.63
Financial Industrial Income $1,000 (800) 525-9831	18.5	.69	26.8	good	hi	.64

NAME/MIN. INVESTMENT	AV. ANN. RETURN	BETA	RISK-ADJ. RETURN	PERF. IN "DOWN" MKT.	DIVERS.	EXP. %
Founders Income $250 (800) 525-2440	14.1	.55	25.6	good	hi	1.50
Safeco Income $200 (800) 426-6730	15.9	.79	20.1	fair	hi	.63
Value Line Income $250 (800) 223-0818	18.9	.61	30.1	fair	lo	.78

SPECIALIZED FUNDS

NAME/MIN. INVESTMENT	AV. ANN. RETURN	BETA	RISK-ADJ. RETURN	PERF. IN "DOWN" MKT.	DIVERS.	EXP. %
Century Shares Trust $500 (Insurance and Banking) (617) 523-6844	15.8	.84	18.8	good	lo	.94
Energy Fund $250 (Energy resources) (212) 850-8300	17.8	.85	20.9	poor	hi	.83
GT Pacific $500 (Asian stocks) (415) 392-6181	7.5	.37	20.3	good	lo	1.40
Medical Technology $1,000 (Health care products) (800) 523-0864	15.0	1.17	12.8	fair	hi	1.46
Nat. Aviation & Technology $500 (Aviation hi-tech) (212) 482-8100	14.6	1.09	13.4	fair	hi	1.17

NAME/MIN. INVESTMENT	AV. ANN. RETURN	BETA	RISK- ADJ. RETURN	PERF. IN "DOWN" MKT.	DIVERS.	EXP. %
PAX World Fund $250 (World economic development) (603) 431-0822	15.8	.94	16.8	poor	hi	1.40
Rowe Price International $1,000 (Foreign stocks) (800) 638-5660	NA	.54	NA	fair	lo	1.14
Rowe Price New Era $1,000 (Natural resources) (800) 638-5660	16.4	1.11	14.8	poor	hi	.68
Scudder International $1,000 (International stocks) (800) 225-2470	13.2	.50	26.4	poor	lo	1.05
USAA Sunbelt Era $1,000 (Sunbelt stocks) (800) 531-8181	NA	NA	NA	NA	NA	1.06
Vanguard Index Trust $1,500 (Tracks S&P 500 index) (800) 523-7025	16.7	.99	16.7	fair	hi	.28

Closed-End Mutual Funds

Most mutual funds promise to buy back your shares for the underlying value of the stocks they represent. "Closed-end" funds work more like ordinary corporations, selling a fixed number of shares to the public. If you want to own them, you must buy them from another owner. If you want to sell them, you must find someone to buy them.

That sounds inconvenient, not to mention expensive: to buy or sell closed-end funds that are traded like stock on the exchanges, you must pay regular brokerage commissions. Why, then, would anyone bother when the open-ended variety can be purchased without sales charges?

You might admire the management skills of one particular closed-end fund. Some have done very, very well in recent years. Or you may be impressed by a specific operational advantage closed-end funds have over their open-ended cousins.

When the stock market is booming and most mutual funds are doing well, investors rush to put their money into open-ended funds. Fund managers are thus under pressure to buy stock at just the time when stock prices are cyclically high. On the other hand, when the stock market sags and there are bargains galore, funds have no money to spend because share redemptions outpace share purchases. Indeed, funds may be forced to sell stock at low prices simply to honor their redemption obligation.

Closed-end funds are immune from all that. They need not buy stock when the market is up, nor sell when the market is down. So in theory—and frequently in practice—closed-end funds can afford to be bargain hunters. And that may be part of the reason that, as a group, the 13 closed-end funds examined by Forbes magazine outearned the open-ended stock funds by an average of five percentage points annually.

Another consideration that can make closed-end funds more—or less—attractive is the discount or premium over the underlying asset value. There is no rule, written or unwritten, that says closed-end funds must trade for the underlying value of the stocks they own. And, in fact, most don't. The trendy ones—the Korea Fund, for example, which invests only in Korean securities—trade for considerable premiums, reflecting the market's enthusiasm for the concept. More often than not, though, the broadly diversified stock funds trade for a discount.

That makes the diversified funds a potential bargain: by

investing in a discounted fund, you get more dividend bang for an investment buck. On the other hand, it means that you are a prisoner of a fickle market's attitude toward closed-end funds. Even if the fund performs well, the market may not choose to recognize that reality by bidding up the price of the fund shares.

The limited group of closed-end funds below have all done well in the past decade. Remember, though, this doesn't mean they will do as well in the next. Before buying one, investigate its investment policies by obtaining a prospectus from the management. And check the weekly listings in *Barron's* or the *Wall Street Journal* under "Publicly Traded Funds." Consider funds selling for considerable discounts from their underlying asset value. Avoid funds that trade for considerably more than asset value.

DIVERSIFIED FUNDS	AVERAGE ANNUAL RETURN OVER LAST TEN YEARS	PERFORMANCE "DOWN" MARKETS
Adams Express (301) 752-5900	18.1	excellent
Baker, Fentress (312) 236-9190	26.9	good
General American Investors (212) 916-8400	22.3	good
The Lehman Fund (800) 221-5350	20.3	good
Source Capital (800) 421-4374	38.2	excellent
Tri-Continental (800) 221-2450	17.6	excellent
SPECIALIZED FUNDS		
Japan Fund Japanese Securities (212) 350-8500	23.2	good
ASA Limited Gold Mining Stocks (212) 754-9375	12.0	fair
Petroleum and Resources Natural Resources (301) 752-5900	20.4	poor

INVESTMENTS WITH A TAX EDGE

SHELTERS THAT LAST

Many people are so furious about taxes that they will do almost anything legal—and sometimes more—to avoid paying them. *In their rush to shelter, they end up with investments that pay stingy returns, or investments that are too risky or too illiquid to suit their needs.* Think before you plunk down your nickels, and then think again.

With that said, look at the conservative case for exploiting tax breaks. In spite of the cuts of the early 1980s, in spite of the dramatic reduction in the top tax brackets, taxes remain steeply progressive in the middle-income range. But what Uncle Sam taketh away from the middle class with the left hand, he restoreth with the right. *First and foremost, there are generous no-strings-attached tax benefits for savings targeted for retirement (see page 143). Make the most of them.* Then, if you have savings left over, consider the pros and cons of these tax-advantaged investments.

TAX-EXEMPT BONDS

First some basics. Interest on bonds issued by state and local governments is exempt from federal tax. So, too, is the interest on bonds sold by government-blessed authorities promoting everything from hydroelectric dams to middle-income housing to industrial development to pollution control to hospitals. Offsetting this virtue is the fact that *tax-exempt bonds pay less interest than taxable bonds of equivalent safety, liquidity, and maturity.* The tables below allow you to make comparisons based on your own 1985 income tax bracket.

Tax-exempt bonds, unlike U.S. Treasury or corporate bonds, are typically issued in "serial" form. A local hospital authority might, for example, issue $2 million in bonds, with $100,000 worth maturing in each of the next 20 years. This convention makes tax-exempts convenient to buy because you can choose the bond you want and then match the maturity to your own needs. But it can make them less convenient to sell because serial bonds fragment the market, making each bond a virtually unique commodity.

Like other bonds, tax-exempts maturing in a year or more typically pay interest twice a year. Before 1983, most tax-exempts were issued in "bearer" form: you (or your bank or broker) clipped a coupon that entitled the bearer to cash on demand. Billions worth of these old bearer bonds are still around and are greatly prized by cocaine dealers, the owners of businesses incorporated in obscure Caribbean islands, and others who put great stake in financial privacy. *If you don't have larceny at heart, however, you may find the need to clip the coupons and guard the bond certificates against loss more of an inconvenience than a benefit.* Today, all tax-exempts come "registered" with your name on them. That makes them useless as a means of, say, passing on assets to grandchildren without paying estate taxes. But it means that interest is automatically mailed to the owner.

Whether they are bearer or registered bonds, many tax-exempts contain a "call" provision giving the issuer the right to buy back the securities at a specified time and price. Thus, the small print on an Atlas-Zeus Dam Authority 10 percent bond, maturing in 2004, may allow the Authority to repurchase the bonds at the original issue price any time after 1988.

The provision works entirely in the favor of the issuer. If interest rates in the economy rise, the Authority will sit on its hands and pay the 10 percent interest until maturity. However, if interest rates were to fall—say to 8 percent in 1990—Atlas-Zeus would probably "call" the bonds and issue new ones paying less interest. And you would end up

SINGLE RETURN*

If your taxable income is:	Your tax bracket is:	To equal these tax-exempt returns: you would have to earn this percentage on a taxable investment:						
		6%	7%	8%	9%	10%	11%	12%
13,430–15,610	20	7.5	8.8	10.0	11.3	12.5	13.8	15.0
15,610–18,940	23	7.8	9.1	10.4	11.7	13.0	14.3	15.6
18,940–24,460	26	8.1	9.5	10.8	12.2	13.5	14.9	16.2
24,460–29,970	30	8.6	10.0	11.4	12.9	14.3	15.7	17.1
29,970–35,490	34	9.1	10.6	12.1	13.6	15.2	16.7	18.2
35,490–43,190	38	9.7	11.3	12.9	14.5	16.1	17.7	19.4
43,190–57,550	42	10.3	12.1	13.8	15.5	17.2	19.0	20.7
57,550–85,130	48	11.5	13.5	15.4	17.3	19.2	21.1	23.1
85,130 plus	50	12.0	14.0	16.0	18.0	20.0	22.0	24.0

*While this book was in production, Congress was considering reforms that would lower the highest tax brackets. If tax rates are changed, the taxable incomes and tax brackets above will be incorrect. Once you've figured your own tax bracket, though, the table will give you the equivalents between taxable and tax-free yields.

JOINT RETURN

If your taxable income is:	Your tax bracket is:	To equal these tax-exempt returns: you would have to earn this percentage on a taxable investment:						
		6%	7%	8%	9%	10%	11%	12%
16,650–21,020	18	7.3	8.5	9.8	11.0	12.2	13.4	14.6
21,020–25,600	22	7.7	9.0	10.3	11.5	12.8	14.1	15.4
25,600–31,120	25	8.0	9.3	10.7	12.0	13.3	14.7	16.0
31,120–36,630	28	8.3	9.7	11.1	12.5	13.9	15.3	16.7
36,630–47,670	33	9.0	10.5	11.9	13.4	14.9	16.4	17.9
47,670–62,450	38	9.7	11.3	12.9	14.5	16.1	17.7	19.4
62,450–89,090	42	10.3	12.1	13.8	15.5	17.2	19.0	20.7
89,090–113,860	45	10.9	12.7	14.6	16.4	18.2	20.0	21.8
113,860–169,020	49	11.8	13.7	15.7	17.7	19.6	21.6	23.5
169,020 plus	50	12.0	14.0	16.0	18.0	20.0	22.0	24.0

with your money back and no place to invest it that would pay an equally secure 10 percent.

It's important, then, to read the fine print and, where possible, avoid bonds with call provisions. An alternative strategy is to buy bonds selling well below the call price so there is little likelihood that the call provision will ever be exercised.

Medium- and long-term tax-exempts can be bought and sold in $5,000 denominations. Bonds issued for a year or less (in discount form, like Treasury bills—see page 43) usually come in $100,000 minimums. Both types are traded through full-service brokerage houses, specialized bond dealers, and, in some cases, banks. A few cities, notably Boston, have sold mini-bonds in denominations as small as $100 direct to civic-minded residents.

Regardless of their denomination, bond prices are quoted on a base of 100. A bond with a face value of $5,000 that actually sells for $5,000 would be quoted at a price of 100. If the price declines to 93½, it can be had for $4,675 (93.5 percent of $5,000 equals $4,650). Unless a price is quoted as "flat," a buyer is also obliged to pay the seller any unpaid interest, calculated to the day of the purchase.

Brokers rarely charge commissions for trading tax-exempt bonds. But that should be no comfort since sales charges are hidden in the difference between what brokers pay for bonds and what they sell them for. This indirect commission is usually about 2½ percent on heavily traded issues available from virtually any dealer. *But it could be much higher— as high as 10 percent—if you are in a hurry to sell a small number of bonds issued by, say, an obscure school district or pollution control authority.*

Safety

Not long ago, virtually all tax-exempt bonds were backed by the taxing power of a government. If a community defaulted on one of these "general obligation" bonds, a judge could, at least in theory, order local taxpayers to ante up the interest and principal. Now most tax-exempts are "revenue" bonds, backed only by the revenues of the hospital or power dam or house mortgages being financed with the money.

General obligation bonds seem safer, and they often are. But in some cases, the revenues from a tax-exempt authority are so secure that the bonds are very safe—perhaps safer than the bonds of a heavily taxed community facing hard times. For example, homeowners with the cheap mortgages that back an issue of housing authority bonds will be extremely reluctant to default on their mortgage payments. And in the occasional case where a homeowner is forced to default, the underlying value of the houses should cover most or all of the debt.

Since the mid-1970s, an increasing proportion of tax-exempts have been issued with private insurance covering the timely payment of interest and repayment of principal. The insurance, of course, is only as good as the credit of the insurance company or consortium of insurance companies that issues the policy. But the credit of the four principal insurers—the Municipal Bond Insurance Association (MBIA), Ambac, the Financial Guaranty Insurance Corporation (FGIC), and Bond Investors Guarantee (BIG)—is very good indeed. *It would take a general economic catastrophe exceeding the severity of the Great Depression to knock these insurers into default.*

If a bond does not carry private insurance, the only practical way for a small investor to judge its riskiness is to look at the credit rating from one of the two major rating agencies. Moody's and Standard and Poor's assign risk according to the following scales of quality:

	MOODY'S	STANDARD AND POOR'S
Best	Aaa	AAA
Excellent	Aa	AA
High	A	A
Medium	Baa	BBB
Speculative	Ba	BB
Low	B	B
Poor	Caa	CCC
In or near default	Ca	CC
Lowest Grade	C	C

Individuals who buy tax-exempts are a conservative breed. Most are in love with the AAA/Aaa ratings held by bonds that are privately insured or are collateralized by U.S. Treasury securities or are linked to the credit of a very healthy state government. But risk of default should be put in perspective. With the exceptions of the special "put" and "floating rate" bonds discussed later, all bonds are subject to fluctuations in value as interest rates in the economy rise and fall. *And the risk of default is much smaller for a long-term bond with a "medium" Baa/BBB rating than the risk of losing resale value through interest rate increases on a AAA/Aaa bond.*

Moreover, the ratings themselves are fallible. It may be true, for example, that a general obligation bond issued by the State of California deserves an AAA rating today because very little of the state's potential taxing power goes into the service of debt. But no one can really predict the outcome of the sort of crisis in which a state government would default. For all we know, a bankruptcy judge in a lower-rated state like Pennsylvania might be tougher on the taxpayers than a judge in California. The backing behind a revenue bond is usually more tangible and thus easier to measure.

Still, there is more art than science to the rating systems. So if it helps you to sleep better, stick with A-rated bonds or better. *But if you can bear a little risk, BBB/Baa bonds may be sufficiently rewarding in extra interest to make the gamble worthwhile.*

Yield

With rare exceptions, the interest on tax-exempt bonds is below the yield available from taxable Treasury or corporate bonds of equivalent safety. That's to be expected: the only reason state and local authorities issue tax-exempt bonds is to save on interest costs. But it does mean that investors must have some idea about their present—and future—tax brackets in order to figure whether tax-exempts are right for them.

One critical factor to any analysis of the attraction of tax-exempts is just how much lower tax-exempt rates are than taxable. In recent years, rates on long-term tax-exempts—those maturing in ten years or more—have edged closer to their taxable counterparts. *Thus, even average-income families may benefit from owning them, provided they are willing to put up with the inferior liquidity of most issues.* This is not the case, though, with short-term tax-exempts, a market dominated by high-bracket corporate and individual investors. Here, yields average only about half the taxable yield, so it's hard to gain much of an income edge unless you're close to the 50 percent tax bracket.

State and local taxes have been ignored in these calculations. For example, a New York City resident who buys tax-exempts issued anywhere in New York State gets a triple whammy in the form of exemption of state and local income taxes as well as federal. But note that *most states do tax the interest earned on bonds from other states.* Only bonds from Puerto Rico and Guam get tax-exempt treatment, no matter where the owner resides.

TAX SWAP

It's as predictable as the turning of the leaves in New England. Each October, the financial pages of every big city newspaper are full of ads for "tax swaps" promising what amounts to a free lunch for investors in tax-exempt bonds. Lunch isn't quite free. *However, if you happen to own tax-exempts that are now worth less than you paid for them, a tax swap may suit you.* Here's how it works under the 1985 tax laws:

Say you paid the full $10,000 face value years ago for some long-term bonds paying 8 percent, or $800 a year. Since the purchase, suppose interest rates in the economy have risen sharply; now bonds like yours paying $800 a year are worth only $8,000. Suppose you now sell the bonds for their $8,000 market value and immediately reinvest the proceeds in other bonds of roughly the same quality and maturity date.

The new bonds should produce about the same amount of income each year. But you will have sold bonds that cost $10,000 for just $8,000, thereby generating an income tax deduction.

The $2,000 paper loss can be used to reduce your tax liability. If, for example, you've sold other securities this same year for more than you paid for them, the $2,000 loss can offset $2,000 in long-term capital gains. If you don't have any capital gains, you can still use the loss to offset half as much ordinary income—in this case, $1,000.

What's the catch? For one thing, it costs money to swap bonds. The fees for buying or selling tax-exempts is hidden in the difference between the amount dealers will pay for a bond and what they will sell it for. *But the net cost of the "round-trip" sale and purchase in a tax swap is typically 3 to 5 percent of the principal.*

For another, the IRS could disallow the paper loss generated in the swap if it decides the securities sold and bought are too much alike. *Be sure that the new bonds differ from the old in some significant way— a different maturity date, perhaps, or a different coupon rate.*

Probably the most important point to keep in mind is that a tax swap doesn't create the loss—the rise in interest rates did that. It merely permits you to time the realization of the loss for purposes of minimizing income taxes. Don't let a bond dealer bully you into a swap that costs you hundreds of dollars in hidden commissions, but doesn't happen to meet your own tax-planning goals.

Choosing the Right Tax-Exempt Bond

Yield and safety from default are primary considerations. But other factors should count, too. *The longer the term of a bond, the more its value will decline, should interest rates in the economy* go up. Then there's the question of liquidity. Unless you are pretty sure you want to hold a bond until it matures (or is called), consider only "brand-name" bonds— general obligations of large states with good credit, or revenue bonds from big, secure projects such as turnpikes. Such bonds can be sold relatively easily at any time. And if you don't expect to hold the bond for at least a few years, don't buy at all: the minimum round-trip cost of buying and selling $5,000 or $10,000 worth of the most liquid general obligation bonds is usually 3 or 5 percent.

It may also make sense to investigate some of the alternatives to traditional long-term tax exempts.

Prefunded or fully collateralized bonds. Some authorities with relatively poor credit have sold bonds backed, dollar for dollar, by U.S. Treasury bonds, U.S. Government-guaranteed housing bonds, or letters of credit from giant banks. That, of course, makes them as safe as the underlying guarantor. But the bond market isn't always rational—a bond linked to Puerto Rico, for example, typically commands premium interest regardless of the collateral behind it. Sometimes, too, the market will ignore the fact that bonds originally issued without special collateral often acquire it over time, as authorities accumulate cash to pay them off long in advance of maturity. They're worth looking for.

Zero coupon bonds. Like zero coupon Treasury or corporate securities, zero coupon tax-exempts pay out nothing until maturity, compounding interest at a prescribed rate as they grow in value. As a result, you can figure exactly how much you'll end up with in ten or 20 years without knowing anything about interest rates in the future. That can be handy if you have a specific dollar target to hit—say, a future cash payment as part of a property settlement in divorce. But there are some serious disadvantages. Zeros usually pay less interest than equivalent bonds with the same maturity date. They are less liquid, too, and more subject to fluctuations in value as interest rates change. And, to add insult, some contain call provisions that allow the issuer to redeem them in advance of maturity—and at no profit to you.

Put bonds.   A call provision, of course, lets an issuing authority buy back bonds at its discretion. A "put" bond, or tender option bond, gives you the complementary privilege. At times specified in the bond contract, you get the right to sell the bonds back at a price agreed in advance. *The option to sell means that the bond can never lose much value in the marketplace as long as the credit of the issuer remains strong.* Or at least as long as somebody's credit remains strong: the put provision is often guaranteed by a bank. But there's no free lunch to be had here. Yields on put bonds are always well below equivalent bonds lacking the put feature.

Floating rate bonds.   Rather than providing a fixed annual interest return, the interest on these bonds changes wih some specified index, like current yields on T-bills. That makes the value of floaters less sensitive to changes in interest rates. As with put bonds, their value doesn't fall as interest rates rise. But unlike put bonds, their value doesn't rise when interest rates fall. Floaters can be good investments for people in high tax brackets who simply don't want to take market risks.

Tax-exempt Bonds in Slicker Packages

Brokers love to sell tax-exempt bonds because of the high indirect commissions. But remember, tax-exempts have serious drawbacks. Compared to most stocks and all Treasury bonds, they are illiquid. Moreover, they come in bulky sizes that make it difficult for small- and medium-size investors to diversify holdings. *Unless you have a fairly large amount of money—$25,000 or more—and the patience to lock up your investment for at least five years, individual tax-exempt bonds probably aren't right for you.* But that doesn't mean you can't reap the rewards of tax-exempts in other forms.

Tax-exempt unit trusts.   This is one terrific idea. An investment company or bond department within a brokerage house buys several million dollars worth of tax-exempts, splitting the sum among ten to 20 different issues. Then the company creates a trust with the bonds as the assets and offers shares in the trust for $1,000 each, plus 2 to 5 percent commission. Generally, a brokerage house acts as the selling agent. You can find its ads in the *Wall Street Journal* and the business pages of most big-city newspapers.

A $1,000 unit in a trust represents ownership of a few dollars worth of each of many different bonds. The communities and authorities issuing the bonds pay interest to the sponsor of the trust, who divides it up and mails it to the trust's owners. Similarly, when bonds in the trust mature or are called, the cash is divided among the owners.

Competition has spurred the creation of tax-exempt trusts to meet specialized needs. Some contain only bonds from a single state (New York, Massachusetts, Virginia, Michigan, Pennsylvania, California), so purchasers who are residents are freed from state and local tax obligations. Some are insured. Some contain bonds due to mature in ten years rather than 20 or 30, reducing the risk of capital loss should interest rates rise. Some give owners the right to sell units to a bank at a fixed price, giving them all the virtues of "put" bonds. Some contain a few zero coupon issues mixed in with regular bonds. As a result, you get a little less interest each month but end up with more money than you began with.

Owning units of a tax-exempt bond trust can be much better than owning bonds. First, the investment needed for diversification is smaller. An outlay of $5,000—usually the minimum purchase required by trust sponsors—gets you a piece of many bonds. Second, you need only keep track of payments from a single source. Third, interest payments usually come on a convenient monthly schedule, rather than twice a year. Fourth, trusts are liquid. With rare exceptions, the trust sponsor maintains a standing offer to buy back units at the market price.

It still pays, though, to look carefully at the prospectus before you buy. Sponsors often go for the highest yields, neglecting to consider weaknesses such as poor protection against calls. *Remember, too, that broker commissions on unit trusts are fairly high. If you buy and sell quickly, you will lose money.*

Tax-exempt bond funds.   Another way to buy tax-exempt bonds without risk of tears later on. Unit trusts are fixed packages of bonds that self-destruct when the underlying securities mature or are called. Bond funds are mutual funds that buy and sell bonds on investors' behalf, with the goal of maximizing income and minimizing risk. Thus, a small amount of money—with some funds, as little as $1,000— gets you a piece of a diversified portfolio of bonds. *And since the mutual fund must buy back your shares at any time for their underlying value, your investment is highly liquid.* Bond funds usually give you the option of receiving income on a regular basis or automatically reinvesting it in more shares of the fund. Some offer the convenience of making withdrawals by check, like money market funds.

Some tax-exempt bond funds, generally the ones sold by brokers, charge fees to buy shares. *Stick with the "no-load" funds—the sort marketed directly by the investment companies—in order to reduce selling costs.* The sponsors of no-load funds don't, of course, run them as charities. They charge annual fees for their services, which reduce the net income to shareowners. But there is no question that the costs of owning a no-load fund average out to less.

Making the Choice
Which of the three options—bonds, unit trusts, or funds— is right for you? Skip the bonds unless you know what you're doing, enjoy "hands-on" money management, and have at least $25,000 to invest in bonds alone. Since unit trusts have relatively high sales charges and very low management fees, they are good for people who plan to hold on to the investment for several years. No-load bond funds have no sales charges, so they suit investors who may want to get out relatively quickly. But however you choose to invest in tax-exempt securities, shop around. That advice goes for almost any investment. But it is doubly important with bonds be-

cause the market isn't nearly as competitive as the one for stocks and bonds listed on exchanges.

Tax-Exempts—Where to Buy Them

Every major brokerage house sells some tax-exempt bonds and unit trusts, and, if pressed, can buy any of the ones they don't ordinarily sell on your behalf. But remember, they have far more profit incentive to sell you bonds or unit trusts off their own shelves. It may pay to start with one of these firms that specialize in the tax-exempt market because they carry substantial inventories.

Gabriele, Hueglin and Cashman
(800) 223-2610—outside New York
(212) 422-1700

Kidder, Peabody
(800) 345-8502—outside New York
(212) 510-5446

Lebenthal
(800) 221-5822—outside New York
(212) 425-6116

These tax-exempt bond funds are sold directly, without a load, by the sponsors. Interest yields will differ according to the riskiness of the portfolio, the luck and skill of the managers, and the size of the annual fees.

Dreyfus Tax-Exempt Bond Fund
(800) 645-6561—outside New York
(212) 223-0303

Fidelity High Yield Municipals
(800) 225-6190—outside Massachusetts
(617) 523-1919

Nuveen Municipal Bond Fund
(800) 621-7210—outside Illinois
(312) 621-2067

Oppenheimer Tax-Free Bond Fund
(800) 525-7040—outside New York
(212) 825-4000

Rowe Price Tax-Free Income Fund
(800) 638-5660—outside Maryland
(301) 547-2308

Safeco Municipal Bond Fund
(800) 426-6730—outside Washington
(206) 545-5530

Scudder Managed Municipal Bonds
(800) 225-5163—outside Massachusetts
(617) 328-5000

USAA Tax-Exempt Funds
(800) 531-8181—outside Texas
(512) 690-6062

Value Line Tax-Exempt Portfolio—High-Yield Portfolio
(800) 223-0818—outside New York
(212) 522-5217—in New York

Vanguard Municipal Bond Funds
(800) 523-7025—outside Pennsylvania
(800) 362-0530—in Pennsylvania

These no-load funds are exempt from New York or California taxes because they invest only in bonds issued by those specific states (or U.S. trust territories—Puerto Rico and Guam).

Dreyfus California Tax-Exempt Bond Fund
(800) 645-6561—outside New York
(212) 223-0303

Dreyfus New York Tax-Exempt Bond Fund
(800) 645-6561—outside New York
(212) 223-0303

New York Muni Fund
(800) 528-6050—outside New York
(212) 747-9215

These "intermediate-term" bond funds restrict their portfolios to tax-exempt bonds that mature in about ten years. The idea is to earn a higher yield than is available with tax-exempt money market funds but to incur less risk of capital loss than ordinary long-term bond funds.

Fidelity Limited Term Municipals
(800) 225-6190—outside Massachusetts
(617) 523-1919

USAA Tax-Exempt Intermediate Term Fund
(800) 531-8181—outside Texas
(512) 690-6062

Vanguard Municipal Bond Fund—Intermediate Term Portfolio
(800) 523-7025—outside Pennsylvania
(800) 362-0530

This tax-exempt fund, available from brokers, charges a load of about 5 percent. That would disqualify it from the list, were it not for one special feature. Like most funds, it buys long-term bonds to get the most interest. But unlike the others, it uses fancy hedging techniques to reduce the risk of rapid fluctuations in value that are inherent in long-term, fixed return securities. The fund is too new to have much of a track record. Check a recent prospectus to see how well it's done before even considering a $5,000 minimum purchase.

Principal Preservation Tax-Exempt Fund
(414) 334-5521

It is difficult to predict which companies will be selling which sort of tax-exempt bond unit trusts. In 1983 alone, 640 trusts were created, each a little different from the others. But this abbreviated list of bond trust series and their sponsors will give you a place to start looking. Remember that any full-service stockbroker will be able to sell you one or more brands of unit trust. But few will look beyond the "house brand" unless you insist.

First Trust of Insured Municipal Bonds
Clayton Brown and Associates
(312) 641-3300

Hutton Tax-Exempt Funds
E. F. Hutton and Co.
(212) 742-5000 (or call any local E. F. Hutton office)

Insured Municipals—Income Trusts
Van Kampen Merritt, Inc.
(215) 972-0555

Municipal Bond Trusts
Paine, Webber and Co.
(212) 730-5131 (or call any local Paine Webber office)

Municipal Investment Trust Funds
Call any office of Merrill Lynch, Dean Witter,
Prudential-Bache, or Shearson/American Express

Nuveen Tax-Exempt Bond Funds
John Nuveen and Co.
(212) 668-9500

Sears Tax-Exempt Investment Trusts
Dean Witter Reynolds, Inc.
(212) 524-3630

DEFERRED FIXED ANNUITIES

Don't let the name throw you. *A deferred fixed annuity is simply a savings plan with tax advantages* that happens to be run by a life insurance company and backed by its assets. You deposit (invest) a minimum of $5,000 at an interest rate guaranteed for several months or years by the sponsoring insurance company. The shorter the period of the guarantee, the higher the rate. Generally, the interest is about a percentage point below the yield on long-term U.S. Treasury bonds. Taxes are deferred on the interest income until you make a withdrawal. Should you care to, the money accumulated in the account can be used to purchase an annuity from the sponsor, which pays a guaranteed sum each month for life.

Sounds terrific, and it is. But there are drawbacks. *Deferred annuities should be considered only by investors who expect to keep their funds in the account for at least five years.* Your money is always available on short notice, and the principal value does not change as interest rates fluctuate in the economy. But the sponsor will exact a penalty for early withdrawals. Typically, the penalties start big and diminish with time, beginning at about 7 percent for withdrawals in the first year and disappearing entirely after the seventh. Most policies do offer an escape clause, though: if the interest rate offered falls below some specified minimum, the penalties are waived.

Uncle Sam isn't any happier about premature withdrawals from annuities than sponsors. Money withdrawn from a deferred annuity before ten years have elapsed is subject to a special 5 percent tax beyond ordinary income taxes owed. If, for example, you were in the 34 percent bracket the year you made a withdrawal, you would pay tax on the income at a rate of 39 percent. The 5 percent penalty, incidentally, is waived if you've become disabled or have reached age 59½.

Since they are backed by the assets of regulated life insurance companies, deferred fixed annuities were long considered to be almost as safe as government-insured bank accounts. Then the single largest seller of deferred annuities—the Baldwin-United Corporation—went bankrupt, leaving insufficient cash to cover withdrawals or maintain the high interest rates guaranteed in the annuity contracts. The actual losses to depositors have not proved to be all that large; *owners will eventually get all their money back, plus about two-thirds the expected interest.* But the episode shook the industry and dramatically cut sales.

Obviously, deferred annuities are not as safe as government-insured accounts. *But the deferred annuities still being sold by insurance companies are very safe, and it is very unlikely that there will be a repeat of the Baldwin-United fiasco.* To be doubly safe, though, ask whether the insurer offering a particular annuity is licensed to do business in New York or California. These two states have particularly strict regulation of life insurance companies.

Deferred annuities are sold by life insurance agents and brokerage houses. Prospective buyers should shop for the best terms. But it's worth considering the possibility that annuities sold through big brokerage houses have a slight safety advantage. Rather than risk legal battles or a loss of public confidence, the brokerage houses that sold Baldwin-United annuities contributed substantial sums to settlements of claims by policyholders.

VARIABLE ANNUITIES

Most deferred annuities offer a guaranteed interest yield and are backed by the security holdings of the sponsoring insurance company. You may not know exactly how much you'll make over the years, but it is almost certain to track interest rates in the economy.

Not so with variable annuities, also sold by insurance companies through insurance agents. *These are really mutual funds that operate behind tax barriers.* Your money (typically a $5,000 minimum) is lumped together with others' and invested in stocks or bonds or whatever the prospectus calls for. Your profit (or loss) is determined by the luck and skill of the fund managers.

The clear advantage over an ordinary mutual fund with similar investment policies is that your income tax liability is deferred as long as your money remains in the pot. The clear disadvantage is that premature withdrawals are penalized both by the insurance company sponsor and by the IRS. The subtler disadvantage is that insurance companies have not in the past proved to be particularly good at managing stock and bond portfolios.

The following variable annuities have pretty good track records over the last few years. *Most are run in conjunction with a family of mutual accounts, which makes it possible to switch your money back and forth from a stock to a bond to a money market portfolio without incurring tax liability or paying additional sales charges. It's absolutely essential,* though, to read the prospectus before plunking down your cash. Most of these companies, by the way, will have local agents or sales representatives in your own city. If not, call the numbers listed below.

COMMON STOCK PORTFOLIOS

CG Variable Annuity II
Connecticut General Life
(203) 726-6000

FVL Growth Fund
First Variable Life Insurance
(501) 661-1500

Franklin Life Variable Annuity B
Franklin Life Insurance
(217) 528-2011

Value Line Centurian Fund
Guardian Life Insurance
(212) 598-8259

FIXED INCOME PORTFOLIOS

Massachusetts Mutual Variable Annuity 2
Massachusetts Mutual Life Insurance
(413) 788-8411

NWNL Select Variable Account—High Yield Fund
Northwestern National Life Insurance
(612) 372-5605

Prudential Individual Variable Accounts
Prudential Insurance
(602) 264-7892

U.S. SAVINGS BONDS

Just kidding, right? Everybody knows U.S. Savings Bonds are a bad deal. Safe, maybe. And good for kids' birthday presents because you can buy one for as little as $25. But, like savings accounts at banks, not to be taken seriously by adults who want to make the most from their money.

Well, "everybody" is wrong. Savings Bonds were a bad investment, but no longer. Since the program was reformed in 1982, series EE bonds have offered an attractive alternative for very conservative investors who don't particularly value liquidity and who are in a high enough tax bracket to benefit from the modest tax advantages.

Like the old EE bonds, the new ones are sold in $25 multiples at banks or through payroll deductions. But the interest rate is no longer fixed. Instead, anyone who holds on to a bond for at least five years is paid a rate equal to 85 percent of the average yield on five-year Treasury notes.

The rate is adjusted and credited every six months. But regardless of what happens to the Treasury note rate, owners are guaranteed a minimum of 7.5 percent interest for the nominal ten-year life of the bonds. So if Treasury note rates happen to average 12 percent, you get 85 percent of 12 percent, or 10.2 percent. If Treasury note rates should slip to 7 percent, you get the 7.5 percent minimum. No one, by the way, expects this guaranteed minimum to be suspended once the ten years have expired. With past series of Savings Bonds, the original terms were honored by Washington for up to 40 years.

Savings Bonds carry with them some significant tax breaks. Like other U.S. Government securities, interest cannot be taxed by states or localities. The interest is not taxed by the Feds, either, until the bonds are cashed in.

This latter advantage can add up to real money. Say, for purposes of comparison, you invested $10,000 in a ten-year bank certificate of deposit paying 10 percent, compounded twice annually. Assume, too, that you were in the 40 percent tax bracket so that each year you would have to pay taxes equal to 40 percent of the interest income. You would end up with $18,061.

Now try the experiment again, this time investing $10,000 in series EE bonds that, on average, happened to pay the same 10 percent rate. If you cashed the bonds after the same ten years, you would receive $26,533. And after paying taxes on the interest, you would still have $19,920, or 23 percent more in after-tax interest earnings! In real life, the advantage can be even greater. People's tax brackets fluctuate, typically falling sharply after retirement. By timing redemptions of Savings Bonds for years in which taxable income is low, owners can do even better.

The one (very long) string attached to Savings Bonds is the need to hold them for substantial periods. For the first six months after purchase, there is no way to redeem a Savings Bond. Redeem one in the seventh to twelfth month, and you receive only 5.5 percent interest. Thereafter, the rate increases by a quarter percentage point every sixth month until five years have passed. Only after five years are you entitled to 7.5 percent or the average rate on Treasury notes, whichever is greater.

U.S. Savings Bonds, then, serve much the same function as the deferred annuities sold by life insurance companies. They can be expected to pay about a percentage point less interest. And the financial penalties for withdrawal within five years are greater. But these significant disadvantages may be outweighed by a number of advantages. Savings Bonds come in much smaller units. They are sold (and can be redeemed) with a minimum of paperwork. They are guaranteed by the U.S. Government. And a withdrawal between the fifth and tenth year does not subject you to tax penalties.

TRUSTS AND GIFTS TO KIDS AND PARENTS

Practically everybody knows that tax-exempt bonds can raise after-tax income. And sophisticated investors understand that the same goals can be reached through a variety of tax-deferral methods. But a surprisingly small number of Americans take advantage of another route to tax reduction: transferring taxable income to family members in lower tax brackets.

The plans can be complicated; the underlying idea is simple. Income you spend on your kids' tuition or parents' retirement condo is taxed at your—presumably high—rate. But income your dependents spend on the same tuition or the same condo is taxed at their—presumably lower—rates. *So a legal device that transfers income from you to them, or, similarly, transfers tax deductions to the family members with the most taxable income, can increase the family's total after-tax income.*

It used to be easy to manage such income transfers using a device called an "interest-free Crown loan." You lent money to little Isabelle at no interest. The kid (or more likely you, on her behalf) invested the money in safe, high-yield securities, such as Treasury bills. Then Isabelle paid any tax owed at her very low tax rate and used the proceeds to pay tuition or spend the summer in Greece. When her own income grew, or you simply got tired of paying her bills, you called the loan.

Since 1984, however, this loophole has been narrowed to needle-eye dimensions. It's still perfectly legal to make an interest-free loan to a dependent. But the IRS now treats interest the dependent earns on the loan as your income, not the child's, unless the sum is $1,000 a year or less.

Exit the Crown loan. Enter the custodial account. Here, each parent may make a tax-free gift of up to $10,000 ($20,000 for two parents) each year to a minor, placing the money in a bank or brokerage account controlled by the parents. That successfully transfers the tax liability to the minor child. But it has two glaring drawbacks.

First, the money—principal as well as interest—becomes the property of the child. So you can never get it back unless Isabelle chooses to give it back. Second, when she reaches age 18 (or in somes states, 21), parents lose any legal say in how the income is spent. So cash that may have been intended to pay for a year at Stanford Medical School might end up financing a year on the beach at Malibu.

That leaves a last (and often best) alternative for transferring income: the "Clifford" trust. Named after George Clifford, the person who established the legal precedent, a Clifford trust is simply a trust arrangement that self-destructs in ten years or more and returns the principal to the donor. You deposit money or securities in the trust, naming your child as beneficiary and you (or another responsible person) as trustee. If you wish, you may even borrow back the money in the trust, paying interest at market rates. *Trust income spent on the beneficiary is taxed at the beneficiary's rate.*

If the trust retains income, the trust itself pays income tax, presumably at low rates.

There are drawbacks. Any capital gain (as opposed to ordinary income) earned by the trust is taxed at the donor's rate, not the trust's. Parents must pay gift tax if they deposit more than $32,550 a year in the trust.* Donors can't, under any circumstances, reclaim their principal for at least ten years after the last deposit. So if you fund the trust over a period of five years, the trust must linger on for at least 15. Trust income must be spent on optional goodies for the kids, such as education or other enlightening activities, not basic living expenses that are the clear responsibility of parents. College tuition or training expenses for the Olympics are okay; dinner with the family at Wendy's isn't.

Setting up the trust is the first step; deciding what assets to put in it is the second. Growth stocks would be a foolish choice because much of the potential earnings would come from capital gains and thus are not eligible for favored tax treatment within the trust. So, for obvious reasons, would real estate or any other investment that would be sheltered from taxes outside the trust. Zero coupon securities (see pages 65 and 105) would make sense only if you also plan to deposit cash in the trust to pay its annual tax bills. *The most conservative choice would be government-insured certificates of deposit or blue chip stocks paying high dividends.* The most flexible would be a loan back to the donor: that approach provides all the tax breaks without depriving you of the use of the money.

Perhaps the most serious impediment to taking advantage of this tax break is the fuss and legal expense—setting up the trust, making sure that the legal conditions are honored, filing the necessary tax returns each year. Clifford trusts aren't high finance—any competent lawyer should be able to cope. *But the initial legal fees and the ongoing need for help from an accountant may negate much of the financial benefit of the trust arrangement.*

Citibank of New York has pioneered a way around this obstacle. It offers a standardized Clifford trust called the

---

*That's right, $32,550. Ours is not to reason why.

"University Trust I." You make a single donation of $10,000 or more, naming Citibank as trustee. In theory, it's up to the bank to decide where the money is invested. In practice, the bank, in advance, gives you a choice of either government-insured CDs or one of the stock or bond funds run by the bank's trust department. When you want the beneficiary to have some of the income, you inform the bank. Assuming the purpose fits guidelines established in advance, the bank complies. The principal reverts to the donor after ten years and one month (or a longer period, established in the trust agreement).

There is no charge for setting up a University Trust. But Citibank currently assesses an annual fee of 1 percent of the amount in the trust, or $250, whichever is greater. That's not much for a trust that has accumulated, say, $50,000. But $250 represents 4 percent of the $10,000 minimum, which could fully offset the tax advantages offered by the trust arrangement.

The net savings depend, of course, on the size and earnings of the trust, the tax brackets of the donor and beneficiary, and the length of the trust. An example, prepared by Citibank, suggests that the savings on an initial investment of $20,000 can indeed be substantial. The bank compares a simple, unsheltered savings plan earning a conservative 10½ percent a year with a ten-year-plus-one-month trust earning the same interest rate. It also assumes that the beneficiary has no other income.

	UNSHELTERED SAVINGS DONOR'S TAX BRACKET			TRUST ALTERNATIVE
	33%	42%	50%	
Total Interest Earnings	$31,010	$29,591	$28,392	$33,102
Less				
Taxes	10,233	12,248	14,196	3,498
Trustee Fees	—	—	—	3,371
Net Earnings	20,777	17,163	14,196	26,233
Net Annual After-tax Return	7.4%	6.4%	5.5%	8.7%

For a donor in the 50 percent bracket, interest income after taxes and fees is nearly doubled. The benefits are less spectacular for donors in lower brackets, but still pretty good. Remember, too, that a no-frills Clifford trust, managed by the donor, could return even more because total fees would be much smaller.

For information about the University Trust, write Citibank; 641 Lexington Avenue; Fourth floor; New York, New York 10043. Or call (212) 319-1702. By the time you read this, other banks or brokerage houses may be offering competitive plans. If you live in a large city, try phoning a few of them to find out.

HOUSING GIFTS

Housing offers another simple, conservative option for shifting assets and tax liability from one family member to another in order to increase family income.* Say your parents are retired. Typically, they will be at a stage in their lives when they will no longer have a mortgage on their home. Even if they do, they will probably not be able to take maximum advantage of the deductibility of mortgage interest because they are in a low tax bracket.

Now, suppose your parents sell the house to you, then rent it back at a monthly figure that is close to the open market rate. If they are over the age of 55 and do not realize a capital gain on the sale that exceeds $125,000, the transfer will not create any tax liability. But once you own the house, you can begin to deduct any excess of mortgage interest over rental income. Better still, you can begin to depreciate the house like any other piece of commercial real estate, deducting thousands of dollars more each year from your taxable income.

The potential advantages of this arrangement turn on a number of factors. Much, of course, depends on your tax bracket and theirs—the greater the difference, the larger the

*This whole strategy is vulnerable to contemplated tax reforms. If a major tax reform package is passed by Congress in 1985, check with an accountant to make sure it still works.

family gain. *If your parents have a low-interest mortgage that can't be transferred with the sale, you may end up losing rather than gaining.* Remember, too, that by taking on mortgage debt, you could reduce your ability to borrow money for other purposes.

The trick that works with retired parents can sometimes also work with children. For example, rather than paying dormitory fees or apartment rental for a student living away from your home, consider the alternative of buying a small house or condo. Deductible mortgage interest will, presumably, more than offset the taxable income you receive as rent. The net advantage will come in the form of depreciation on the property that reduces your taxable income.

Before you attempt any sort of housing shuffle, work through the numbers with care. Be sure not to neglect the implicit cost of any down payment you make. If, for example, you put down $20,000, you have lost the earning power of that $20,000—perhaps $2,000 a year after taxes—until you sell the house. And once you decide that the shuffle makes financial sense, it probably would still pay to invest a few hundred dollars for an analysis by an experienced accountant.

PRECIOUS METALS

THE RAINY DAY PLAY

Is buying gold or silver, or more exotic precious metals such as platinum and palladium, a way to get rich? Plenty of people have hit it big in the past by mortgaging their underwear to buy that last gram. And there is, apparently, an infinite supply of investors who want to believe it can happen again. Dozens of "insider" newsletters serve these investors with endlessly recycled predictions of $2,000 an ounce gold or $200 an ounce silver by 1990.

Maybe the gold bugs are right; maybe the price of gold will soon take off for the stars. Or maybe it will soon join the S.S. *Titanic* at the bottom of the North Atlantic trench. Nobody knows. And anybody who claims to know either has something to sell or is playing with less than a full deck.

But those harsh words are hardly the end of the story. Even if the prices of previous metals can't be predicted, the factors that send prices up or down are, more or less, understood. And while it's not in everyone's interest to buy precious metals, there's a solid case for limited holdings as part of a diversification program.

GOLD

Gold is mined in a dozen countries including the United States, Canada, Mexico, and Australia. But the lion's share comes from South Africa, which has the richest ores in the most plentiful supply. The other big player in the gold market, the Soviet Union, has a lot of ore of less certain quality. Its exports apparently have more to do with the need to earn hard currencies in the West than with the economics of production.

A lot of the newly mined gold goes into electrical equipment, where it is prized as an excellent conductor that is impervious to corrosion. A lot more ends up in traditional places, like jewelry, dental crowns, and peasants' mattresses. But gold is special. It can't be analyzed like other commodities, where changes in industrial growth rates or weather or production costs offer clues to what will happen to prices.

Accumulated reserves of this virtually indestructible metal far exceed current output, so decisions to sell gold from existing stocks can have more impact on price than the ebb and flow of production. And since the primary use for gold is as a store of value (and much of it is stored by governments), there is no simple way to analyze demand. *What people will pay for gold is largely based on what they think other people will pay for gold in the future, which in turn depends on what they think still others will pay . . .* You get the idea.

We do have a fair sense, though, about what has led to the big ups and downs in gold prices in the recent past. One factor is interest rates: the higher the real (that is, inflation-adjusted) rate, the lower the price. That's because those who buy gold must forego ownership of other assets that pay interest or dividends. Invest $1,000 in a bank deposit paying, say, 12 percent, and you'll end up with almost $2,000 in six years. So anyone who buys gold instead of bank CDs is implicitly assuming that gold prices will, at the very least, double within six years.

Another factor affecting gold prices is political instability. When rich people in poor countries fear for their property, they convert as much of their assets as possible into liquid, portable, untraceable, universally accepted form. Gemstones, such as diamonds, fit the description. But gold fits it better because value is much easier to measure.

Finally, there is the expectation of inflation. In inflationary environments, people naturally flee from assets that are fixed in nominal value. Land serves as an inflation hedge in countries with stable property rights. But in places where inflation feeds fears that property will be confiscated, buying gold is the traditional way to protect wealth.

Americans have to be a touch paranoid to take such disaster scenarios to heart. Nobody is about to overthrow their government or expropriate their bank accounts. Inflation is a more plausible worry. But, in itself, the depreciating dollar is not an adequate reason to buy gold. For unless the rate of inflation exceeds interest rates—a rare and short-lived event in American history—*the surest way to preserve capital is to buy short-term, interest-bearing government securities such as Treasury bills.*

If it is impossible to say whether gold is undervalued or overvalued, if Americans have little cause to fear the political catastrophe that would make gold the only certain store of value, why buy it?

Because gold is a foul weather friend: *when other assets are collapsing in value, gold is likely to rise.* No middle-income American should put a high percentage of his or her assets into mellow yellow. But putting 10 to 15 percent of one's portfolio into gold (or alternatives discussed later) can be defended as a form of asset insurance.

How to Buy Gold

The favorite way to buy gold is in bullion form—coins, medallions, ingots. The advantage of possessing the real thing (as opposed to a piece of paper certifying you own gold) is that you can stare at it, touch it, or run off to Tahiti with it. But before you plunk down your greenbacks, consider the disadvantages.

In many states, the purchase of bullion is subject to sales tax. Wherever you buy bullion and whatever form you buy it in, you'll pay a markup over the value of the metal content. These latter charges can range from 1 to 2 percent for large purchases of coins from the best dealers, to as much as 10 or 15 percent for a single medallion or ingot coin from a local store or mail-order house.

Bullion must be stored and perhaps insured. That may be a minor problem with a cache of ten or 15 coins that fits nicely in the smallest safe deposit box. It can be a headache with one of those 400-ounce bars you see in the movies.

Just because it's yellow and soft doesn't mean it's gold—or at least as much gold as claimed. Fraud is unlikely if you buy popular coins from a major dealer, but it is always a risk.

Privately struck medallions commemorating everything from the Fort Lauderdale Olympics to Famous Desserts Thru the Ages are the worst buys: the premium over the actual gold value is the highest, the problem of establishing resale value most difficult. Companies that sell such medallions in "limited editions" claim that they will gain value as collectors items. Don't bet on it.

Ingots range from 400-troy-ounce bars down to half-ounce wafers. The larger sizes—those above ten ounces—often sell for modest premiums. But they are not terribly liquid, so you may have to settle for considerably less than gold value if you need to sell one in a hurry.

That leaves bullion coins—not to be confused with gold currency coins, such as American $20 gold pieces, that are valued for their scarcity and physical perfection rather than for their weight in metal. Most bullion coins contain one ounce, or close to one ounce, of gold. South Africa, Mexico, and Canada mint smaller coins. But they should be avoided because they are less liquid and sell at much higher premiums.

Some coins are "legal tender"—that is, currency of the countries in which they are minted. Others are "government restrikes" that do not have this status. The only significant difference is that some states that levy sales taxes on restrikes allow legal-tender coins to be traded tax free.

POPULAR GOLD COINS

	GOLD CONTENT (OZ)	LIQUIDITY	TYPICAL PREMIUM
Austrian 100 Corona	.9802	fair	2%
Canadian Maple Leaf*	1.0000	good	5%
Hungarian 100 Corona	.9802	fair	2%
Mexican 50 Peso	1.2057	fair	2%
Mexican One Ounce*	1.0000	good	5%
South African Krugerrand*	1.0000	good	5%
U.S. Gold One Ounce	1.0000	good	5%

*Legal tender in the country of issue.

The Krugerrand, Mexican One Ounce, Canadian Maple Leaf, and U.S. Gold One Ounce carry the largest premiums because they are best known to the public. The other coins are better buys in terms of gold value. But that advantage can be offset by their poorer liquidity: should you need to sell one, you'll lose more on the transaction.

Nitpickers might consider a few other points:

- The Canadian Maple Leaf is the only 100 percent gold coin. That has proved to be a great advertising gimmick. But their resulting softness makes the coins prone to damage. To preserve their looks and minimize the chance they will have to be assayed before they are sold, Maple Leafs must be stored in the protective cases in which they are shipped.

- The Mexican 50 Peso is relatively illiquid because of its odd size. But the coin itself is by far the handsomest, making it a nicer gift for your favorite gold bug.

- U.S. Gold coins commemorate a different famous American each year. That may make them attractive to buyers who wish to display them, but it may have the negative, long-term effect of limiting their liquidity.

GOLD WEIGHTS AND MEASURES

The weight of gold and other precious metals is measured in "troy" ounces and pounds, not to be confused with the "avoirdupois" weights used for just about everything else:

$$1 \text{ troy ounce} = 1.097 \text{ av. ounces}$$
$$12 \text{ troy ounces} = 1 \text{ troy pound} = 13.164 \text{ av. ounces}$$
$$32.22 \text{ troy ounces} = 1 \text{ kilogram} = 35.274 \text{ av. ounces}$$

Gold purity is measured in karats, as fractions of 24. Coins and ingots range from 21 to 24 karat purity. The gold in jewelry is typically 18 karat (or less) because it has been hardened by alloying it with nickel or copper.

24 karat gold = 100.00 percent gold
22 karat gold = 91.67 percent gold
18 karat gold = 75.00 percent gold

Where to Buy Gold Coins

South African, American, Canadian, and Mexican gold coins
are widely available through banks, numismatic coin dealers, and specialized bullion mail-order houses. *Banks generally charge the lowest premiums over gold content value,
small coin shops the highest.* Deak-Perera, a very large bullion dealer in New York (800-221-5700), usually has good
prices. Call Deak-Perera for a price quote for purposes of
comparison with local dealers. Remember, most states charge
taxes on sales of most gold coins.

Gold Certificates

A gold certificate is a warehouse receipt, a document showing that you own a specific quantity of gold located at a
specific storage site. Full-service brokerage houses, big bullion dealers, and some banks sell gold this way. The program
run by Citibank is typical.

You send Citibank $1,000 or more (Visa and MasterCard
accepted). The bank adds your money to that of other customers and makes a bulk purchase of gold, charging 3 percent extra for its trouble. The gold—owned by you, not the
bank—is then stored and insured for an annual fee of a half
percent of its value. Citibank will sell your gold for you at
any time for a commission of 1 percent. Or, for the same 1
percent fee, it will arrange for you to take possession of the
bullion in a state that does not charge sales tax.

*One big advantage of a certificate over bullion coins is
the lower trading cost.* Not every dealer has fees as low as
Citibank's, but buying and selling gold in certificate form is
sure to be a small fraction of a similar "round trip" in coins.

The other advantage is convenience. Owners need not consider the details of storage, insurance, and assaying on the sale.

Against that, one must weigh the fact that certificates aren't shiny and yellow and cool to the touch. Perhaps more important, one must consider the issue of security: will the gold really be there when you want it? To minimize the chance of fraud, it is best to deal with a name-brand bank or brokerage house. And before you write out a check, make certain that the gold actually becomes your property, not simply a liability of a corporation that might someday go bankrupt.

These dealers in gold certificates have impeccable reputations. Comparison-shop for the lowest commissions.

Citibank Precious Metals Service
New York
(800) 223-1080

E. F. Hutton
Des Moines
(800) 453-9000

Merrill Lynch
New York
(212) 290-0200

Shearson/American Express
Precious Metals Division
New York
(212) 321-7155

Gold Mutual Funds

An alternative to buying bullion is to buy shares in companies that mine gold. A half-dozen South African gold stocks are listed on U.S. exchanges and can be purchased from any broker. So can another dozen companies with gold mine holdings in Canada, the United States, the Philippines, and Australia.

Betting on individual gold stocks is different from betting

on the price of gold. Mines vary in quality, and so do the managements of mining companies. The better way to buy gold mine shares is through a mutual fund, preferably one without a "load" or initial sales charge. Arguably, the fund's managers have the knowledge to make educated judgments about the relative value of gold stocks. And, in any case, *a mutual fund diversifies your ownership across many companies.*

Why buy mutual funds when you can buy the metal? No-load mutual funds are more liquid than coins and cost nothing to buy and sell. The funds, moreover, represent a highly leveraged investment in gold since gold stocks go up (or down) far more rapidly than the price of gold. It's easy to see why.

Consider a hypothetical gold mine containing a million ounces of gold that can be extracted and refined for a cost of $290 an ounce. If the price of gold is $300, those million ounces buried in the ground are worth just $10 an ounce, or $10 million. But suppose the price of gold goes up to $375. The unmined gold is now worth $85 an ounce, or a total of $85 million. So just a 25 percent increase in the price of gold can lead to a 750 percent increase in the value of the mine!

Leverage isn't necessarily a good thing for conservative investors (see page 5). *But in the case of gold, it probably is good because it allows investors to take a defensive position in precious metals with very little commitment of capital.* All things considered, then, relatively small purchases of mutual funds seem to be the best way for conservative investors to buy gold.

These no-load funds invest primarily in gold mine stocks but may supplement their portfolios with holdings of gold, silver, and platinum bullion.

Golconda Investors
(800) 431-6060—outside New York
(800) 942-6911—in New York

Lexington Goldfund
(800) 526-4791—outside New Jersey
(800) 932-0838—in New Jersey

United Services Gold Shares
(800) 531-5777—outside Texas
(512) 696-1234

BREAKING THE SOUTH AFRICAN CONNECTION

Some investors wish to invest in gold but are reluctant to invest in (or buy the exports of) South Africa, the world's dominant gold producer. That makes it more difficult to invest in the metal, but it's still possible.

Among the mutual funds, United Services has an explicit policy of putting most of its assests in South African companies. The others mix their portfolios with Canadian and American shares. But all are at least partially invested in South Africa.

For investors who want to commit $5,000 or more, it would be practical to assemble one's own "mutual fund," buying small amounts of non–South African gold shares. Consider these four large, relatively stable companies, all of which are listed on stock exchanges.

Campbell Red Lake Mines (Canada)
Dome Mines (Canada)
Echo Bay Mines (Canada)
Homestake Mining (United States, Australia)

Gold metal purchased in certificate form is anonymous. It could come from anywhere, and most likely comes from South Africa. The same is true for privately manufactured coins and ingots, as well as coins from nonproducing countries like Hungary and Austria. But government-minted coins from the United States (U.S. Gold), Canada (Maple Leafs), and Mexico (One Ounce and 50 Peso) are native gold.

SILVER

Much of what is true about the economics of gold is also true for silver. Both metals have special industrial uses that make them almost irreplaceable. But both are primarily viewed as a store of value—a "hard money" alternative to currency-denominated securities. As a result, year-to-year variations in the price of silver have little to do with production costs or commercial demand and a great deal to do with investors' perception of where silver prices are heading.

There are some differences, though. Governments own relatively little silver. Overall, public and private holdings of silver are far smaller than holdings of gold. In fact, they were small enough to tempt two Texas billionaires to try to corner the market in 1979. The Hunt brothers failed in this incredible scheme, and the consortium they created lost a ton of money. But in the process, they briefly managed to quadruple the price to $48 an ounce and nearly ruined America's second largest brokerage house. Typically, though, *silver prices track the big swings in gold prices.* For, like gold, silver is considered a hedge against bad times, gaining in value during periods of political instability and inflation.

Silver bullion can be purchased in the form of ingots of coins. Most are stamped ".999 fine" meaning they're 99.9 percent silver. Silver cups, plates, and cutlery marked "sterling" are supposed to be 92.5 percent silver; the other 7.5 percent is copper, used to make the silver objects harder to bend.

Ingot weights run from a standard commercial size of 1,000 troy ounces down to one ounce, or even less. *The smaller the ingot, the larger the premium you are likely to pay over the value of the metal.* These premiums run higher than gold—expect to pay a couple percent (plus commission and maybe sales tax) over the metal value even on very large purchases. Remember, too, that a dollar's worth of silver weighs many times more than a dollar's worth of gold. That means storage, insurance, and assay problems are comparably greater.

One relatively liquid form of silver bullion that never needs assaying is old U.S. silver coins. Prior to 1965, dimes, quarters, and half dollars contained 40 percent silver. Perhaps half of these coins were melted for their metal content during the silver boom of 1979–1980. But you can still easily buy either 90 percent or 40 percent silver in bags containing $1,000 face value of coins.

The bags trade for a slight discount below the value of the silver—this discount reflects the cost of refining the metal alloy to pure precious metal. Some dealers claim that the coins are a good buy because no matter how low the price of silver falls, coins will retain their face value. As a practical matter, though, that's not much protection. *Silver would have to depreciate to about $3 an ounce to make the coins worth more as legal tender than as metal.*

The alternative to purchasing bullion by the bag or ingot is to buy it in certificate form. That beats the problems of storage and security, eliminates sales taxes, and drastically reduces the trading costs. The dealers, banks, and brokers that sell gold certificates generally sell silver certificates as well, and for similarly low commissions.

There are no mutual funds that specialize in silver mine stocks. Indeed, there are very few mining companies that specialize in mining silver; in many cases, silver is simply a by-product in the refinement of copper ore. But three companies substantial enough to be listed on the New York Stock Exchange do derive most of their income from silver: Hecla, Callahan, and Sunshine Mining. *A small investment in each would serve as a substitute for a mutual fund.* Remember that silver mine shares, like gold mine shares, are more volatile in value than the metal. A little goes a long way.

Consider one last way to buy a stake in silver. Sunshine Mining has three series of bonds listed on the New York Bond Exchange, each of which expires in 1995. At maturity, they are redeemable for their $1,000 face value or 50 ounces of silver, whichever is greater. The silver option will be worthless, of course, unless the metal rises to $40 an ounce (the 1980 peak was $48; the 1982 low was $5). But in the meantime, each $1,000-face bond will pay $80 to $85 interest each year.

To purchase silver bullion, bullion certificates, or U.S. silver coins, use the contacts listed under gold. *Don't buy silver through newspaper or magazine ads without carefully checking out the seller.* Better still, stick with the list above. Any stockbroker can buy silver mine stocks or bonds on your behalf. To minimize the commission, use one of the discount brokers listed on pages 82–83.

PLATINUM AND PALLADIUM

These two belong to a group of rare metals (including rhodium, osmium, iridium, and ruthenium) that come from mines in South Africa and the Soviet Union. About 90 percent of production goes for industrial uses. (Both are prized for their resistance to corrosion, their high melting temperatures, and their amazing versatility as chemical catalysts.) The other 10 percent is purchased by investors.

Since a high percentage of the metals is used industrially, one might expect that their price movements would follow patterns of industrial demand. In fact, platinum and palladium prices are as erratic and volatile as gold or silver. *Analysts like to compare platinum's price to gold, arguing that it is a relative bargain when it falls below the gold price benchmark.* They also compare platinum prices to palladium; platinum typically costs about five times as much.

It might be possible to make money by betting on the spreads in price among the three metals. But it is a dangerous game, a game for experts only. Conservative investors should consider buying platinum or palladium solely as hedges against inflation.

Platinum bullion comes in one-ounce, ten-ounce, one-kilo, and 50-ounce ingots. Palladium ingots come in 50-ounce and one-ounce sizes. Both can be purchased from the larger precious metals dealers. However, all the vices of physical possession that apply to gold also apply to platinum and palladium: high purchase premiums, sales taxes, and storage and insurance costs. Platinum and palladium certificates, available from Deak-Perera, the metals dealer (800-221-5700), are more sensible choices.

It's worth remembering, too, that the markets for these metals are much smaller than the market for gold. As a result, they are far less liquid.

HEDGE SECURITIES

HAVING IT BOTH WAYS

One way to limit investment risk is to put your money in securities that are insensitive to market fluctuations—money market funds, bank certificates of deposit, U.S. Savings Bonds, and the like. Another is to buy specialized "hybrid" securities (such as bonds convertible into stock) or to pursue specialized hedging strategies (such as covered option writing) that provide some protection against market risks.

Why bother with these more complicated approaches? *Because investors in hedge securities can have it both ways, reducing risk without giving up the opportunity to earn much more than the "riskless" return.* The big drawback is that hedging strategies require more time and attention on the part of the investor.

CONVERTIBLE SECURITIES

Many companies issue bonds or preferred stock (see page 79) that are convertible into a specified number of shares of common stock by some specified date. And many convertible bonds are traded on the New York and American bond exchanges. They are distinguishable from regular bonds in newspaper listings by the "cv" in the column that would otherwise show the "current yield." Convertible preferred stock has no equivalent symbol to distinguish it from the plain vanilla variety.

As with ordinary fixed income securities, some minimum level of income in the form of interest or preferred dividends is assured. *But unlike fixed income securities, convertibles offer the chance for profit should the stock of the issuing company increase in value.*

If that sounds too good to be true, your hearing is acute. Convertibles do guarantee some minimum income, and they do offer a chance for capital appreciation. *But the price of a reasonable chance of capital gains is lower interest or (on preferred stock) a lower dividend yield.* Just how much lower depends on several factors.

Consider a convertible "debenture" (Wall Street jargon for bond) issued by the Hypo-Thetical Corporation. The Hypo-Thetical convertible comes with an 8 percent coupon, good for $40 interest every six months. Under the terms of the underlying contract, the bond may be converted into 20 shares of Hypo-Thetical common stock any time until the 1995 redemption date.

How much is this Hypo-Thetical convertible worth? *At the very least, it must trade for more than a Hypo-Thetical bond with the same expiration date, paying the same coupon rate that doesn't come with a conversion privilege.* So if Hypo-T happens to have an ordinary 8 percent bond due in 1995, the price of the ordinary bond would naturally be the very least the convertible would sell for. If Hypo-Thetical hasn't made this comparison convenient by issuing an 8 percent bond, investors must make an educated guess based on the current yield of comparably secure bonds paying the same interest. This estimate, by the way, is known as the "investment value" of the convertible.

Note, too, that the convertible can't be worth any less than the value of the common stock for which it can be exchanged at any time. Let's say Hypo-Thetical stock is currently selling for $45 a share. Since the debenture is convertible into 20 shares of common, the "conversion value" is 20 times $45, or $900. In (hypothetical) fact, the convertibles are selling on the East Dropdead, Texas Stock Exchange for $990, a "premium" of 10 percent over the conversion value.

Why would anyone pay this 10 percent premium? Because owners of Hypo-Thetical convertibles are willing to pay something to have it both ways. If the stock were to rise in value by one-third, to $60 a share, the conversion value of the convertible would rise to 20 times $60, or $1,200. And it is highly likely that the convertible would increase in value by roughly the same percentage. On the other hand, if the stock were to fall by one-third, to $30 a share, the convertible would fall much less, at the very least retaining its "investment value." Meanwhile, the owner of the convertible would be partially compensated for his woes with annual interest of $80, about 8 percent on his original investment of $990.

Convertibles, then, aren't something for nothing. How should one decide whether a particular issue is worth owning? To begin with, *never buy a convertible unless there's a good reason to believe that the underlying common stock is a good investment.* That, of course, is not so easy to determine. Most likely you'll have to rely on someone's specific investment advice.

Second, you'll have to make a judgment about how much interest you are willing to sacrifice in return for the chance for capital appreciation. In part, that must be based on your own attitude toward risk. In part, it depends on how a particular issue compares with other convertibles.

If all this sounds slightly discouraging, you're getting the message. *Choosing individual convertible issues is like picking stocks—only more complicated.* For those who like the idea of convertibles but don't want to take the time to do the picking, it's wise to seek specific investment advice from an institution that has nothing to gain or lose from your decisions—that is, not from a broker.

There are two good sources, each of which provides general data and recommends specific issues. Neither source of advice is cheap. But it's better to make the investment in information before committing thousands of dollars to a purchase of securities.

Value Line Options and Convertibles
711 Third Avenue
New York, New York 10017
(800) 223-0818
Price: $34 for 8 weeks, $395 for 52 weeks

RHM Convertible Survey
172 Forest Avenue
Glen Cove, New York 11542
(516) 759-2904
Price: $91.25 for 26 weeks, $166.50 for 52 weeks

COVERED OPTIONS

"Covered" option writing is a strategy for minimizing losses in the event of a fall in securities prices. Before describing the pros and cons of this strategy, take a little time to understand what options are and how they work.

An option is the right to buy or sell shares of stock at a specified price for a specified number of weeks or months. An option to buy is a "call"; an option to sell is a "put." Puts and calls in about 300 different stocks are now traded on four options exchanges, with daily listings in many newspapers. The listings usually look like this:

OPTION & N.Y. CLOSE	STRIKE PRICE	CALLS-LAST			PUTS-LAST		
		DEC	MAR	JUN	DEC	MAR	JUN
ITT							
28	20	8½	9	s	r	r	s
28	25	3¾	4½	5¼	¼	1	1¼
28	30	1⅜	2¾	2⅞	2⅝	3¼	3½
28	35	¼	1	1½	r	r	r
28	40	⅛	s	s	r	s	s

Each of the five International Telephone and Telegraph Company options listed above is the right to buy or sell 100 shares of the stock. The "New York Close" is the closing price of the stock that day on the New York or American Stock Exchange.

The "strike price" is the price at which the holder of the option may sell (in the case of a put) or buy (in the case of a call) the stock in question. Note that five different strike prices, ranging from $20 to $40, are listed for ITT. For some stocks, there will be more, for some, less—the idea is to cover the plausible range of prices at which the stock may sell over the coming months. New strike prices are added when the stock approaches the high or low end of the range.

The numbers following the strike price show the price of the option (known as the "premium") the last time it was traded this day. The dates refer to the expiration date of the option, which occurs on the third Friday of the month. Thus, at the close of the market this day, someone was willing to pay $375 (3¾ × 100 shares) for a December 25 call—that is, the right to buy 100 shares of ITT stock at $25 a share any time between now and the third Friday in December. To secure an option to purchase until March, they would have to pay $450 (4½ × 100). To buy a June 25 call, they would have to pay $525.

"Puts" work the same way. A December 25 put—the right to sell 100 shares of ITT stock at $25 a share any time between now and December—would cost you $25 (¼ × 100 shares). The March 25 put would cost $100; the June 30 put, $350.

Columns with an "r" denote that no trade was made that day. Columns with an "s" denote that no market is being made in this particular option.

Under the rules of the exchanges, option contracts need not be settled by the transfer of the underlying stock. Instead, option sellers can always settle their account for cash by buying back the option at the market price.

Consider the logic that underlies the numbers in these listings. The price of ITT stock is 28. Therefore a call at a striking price of 20 is worth, at the very least, $8 per share because the holder could exchange the call for the stock, sell it, and net $8 a share (neglecting commissions). Investors are willing to pay more for a call than the difference between the current stock price and the strike price because there is the possibility that ITT stock will go up in price. *The longer the period to expiration and the greater the volatility of the stock, the more people will pay.*

Where the current stock price exceeds the strike price—as is the case for the first two ITT options above—the call is "in the money." Where the current price is less than the strike price—the last three ITT options—the call is "out of the money." From the buyer's point of view, "in the money" calls are less risky. There is a smaller chance of losing a lot of money (or making a lot of money) as the stock fluctuates in value. From the point of view of the sellers, "out of the money" calls are less risky. Indeed, a modest increase in the stock price will cost the option seller nothing if the stock price never exceeds the strike price before the expiration of the call.

Puts are options to sell. As with any option, the longer it lasts, the more it's worth. But in other respects, puts are the opposites of calls: the higher the strike price of a put, the more it is worth to the owner.

The big selling point to puts and calls—and the reason the option market caught on so quickly in the 1970s—is the financial leverage they generate.

Suppose you think ITT stock is a good buy, likely to rise from 28 to 40 in the next six months. You could invest $2,800 in 100 shares and, if all goes as expected, sell the shares for $4,000 six months later. The profit (neglecting commissions) would be $1,200.

Suppose instead, you invested $2,700 in June 35 calls for 1,800 shares of ITT stock. If the stock went to 40, the calls would rise from 1½ to 5 (40 minus 35 equals 5). Neglecting commissions, the $2,700 investment would thus end up being worth 5 × 1,800, or $9,000. So rather than settling for a $1,200 profit, you would make $6,300!

The other side of the leverage coin, of course, is greater risk of loss. Suppose ITT stock were still selling for $28 six months from today. The owner of 100 shares of stock would neither have gained nor lost. The owner of June 35 calls would lose every penny.

Some people make a lot of money by purchasing puts and calls. *But no call strategy based on leverage is any better than the underlying predictions about what will happen to the value of the stocks.* So unless you are looking for a way to get rich (or poor) in a hurry and have strong convictions about the stock market, simple options strategies aren't for you.

What may make sense, though, for some investors is to use the sale of call options to reduce risk. Suppose you bought 100 shares of ITT stock for $2,800 and, at the same time, sold a June 30 call for $275. If the price of the stock did not change over the six months, the option would expire without any cost to you. You would end up $275 ahead— and get two quarterly dividends from ITT as well, worth another $50. Indeed, you would break even or better as long as the stock remained above 24¾ (the price of the stock less the income from the call and the dividends).

Many investors routinely write "covered" calls—that is, calls against stock they already own—selling a new call each time the old one expires. Suppose ITT stock never went up or down in value, but the dividend and the premium on six-month calls at 30 remained the same. The annual income (again, neglecting commissions) would come to $650: $550 for the two calls, plus $100 in dividends. That would be equivalent to an annual rate of return of 23 percent on a stock that never changed in value!

If covered call writing is so lucrative, why doesn't everybody do it? For one thing, not all stocks rate premiums large enough to generate such high returns. For another, commissions can eat into the return. Full-service brokers typically charge $25 to buy or sell a single (100 share) option. That's not much for the $275 calls just discussed, but it could be quite a chunk of a call selling at, say, $100. For still another, there are tax drawbacks. The income associated with the capital appreciation of a stock isn't taxed until the stock is sold—and then, it's taxed at the lower, capital gains rate. But the cash received in selling a call is treated as ordinary, fully taxable income.

Most important, though, covered option writing puts a cap on the possible return to your investment in the stock. If you sold calls at 30 on ITT, you would keep any appreciation in the value of the stock up to $30. But any appreciation beyond 30 would go to the owner of the call you've sold. For example, if the ITT stock went from 30 to 35, the stock would gain $500 in value. But the gain would be fully offset by your cost of buying back the call.

Is the increased likelihood of profit worth the loss of potential capital gains? Much, of course, depends on your attitude toward investment risks and your willingness to pay close attention to day-to-day changes in stock prices. If this conservative, sophisticated investment strategy does appeal, consider the following approach:

- Buy several different stocks and write calls against each, using a discount broker to minimize commissions. That will give you some of the advantages of diversification.

- Choose stocks with high premiums, figured as a percentage of the cost of the stock. Such stocks are inherently more volatile. But the yields on covered call writing for low volatility stocks is too small to bother with.

- Write "out of the money" calls—calls in which the strike price is at least 5 percent above the current market price. Among other considerations, that minimizes the likelihood you'll have to cover your position by buying back the call before the expiration date. That will save you the commission on the extra transaction.

- Buy professional advice in choosing the stocks—but don't seek it from a broker. It probably makes sense to use the Value Line Investment Survey (see page 192).

The alternative to writing covered calls yourself is to buy shares in a mutual fund that does it for you. That saves you the trouble of picking the stocks to be optioned and keeping tabs on renewals of the options. It also provides diversification.

The two no-load funds listed below can be expected to do relatively well in down markets and relatively poorly in booming markets.

Analytic Optioned Equity Fund
Minimum Investment: $25,000 (ouch!)
(714) 833-0294

Gateway Option Income Fund
Minimum Investment: $500
(513) 621-7774

INVESTING FOR RETIREMENT

LETTING UNCLE PAY

Don't think of a retirement account as the means to your end.* They are that—but they're much, much more. *Individual Retirement Accounts (for everyone) and Keogh Plan accounts (for the self-employed) are terrific ways to reduce taxes.* Practically everybody with income from employment should have one, even people who are unable to set aside more than they currently manage to save.

INDIVIDUAL RETIREMENT ACCOUNTS

Individual Retirement Accounts, known as IRAs, were originally created by Congress to give wage earners who were ineligible for company pensions a comparable incentive to save. But the law was liberalized in 1981. *Now, anyone who works full time or part time, with a pension plan or without, is welcome to start one.*

Individuals may contribute as much as they like of their first $2,000 in earnings. If you made $200 babysitting in your spare hours, you could put up to $200 in an IRA. Make $2,000, and put away the entire $2,000. That's all, though; even if you made $200,000, the maximum contribution is still $2,000.

Working couples may each contribute up to the $2,000 limit as long as the money goes into separate accounts. A nonworking spouse may have his or her own IRA. *But the combined contributions to the two accounts cannot exceed*

*Sorry about that. Sometimes they just slip out . . .

a total of $2,250. An attempt in Congress to increase this to a total of $4,000 barely failed in 1984. But the limit may have been raised by the time you read this. *If you have doubts, call any bank.*

What makes an IRA so special is that contributions are deductible from your taxable income, even if you don't choose to itemize other deductions. And any taxes on the income earned within your IRA are deferred until you withdraw the money. *This double whammy of deduction and deferral can immensely increase the purchasing power of your savings.*

Consider a taxpayer who must choose between a maximum $2,000 investment in an IRA or setting aside $2,000 for an equivalent nonsheltered investment. Suppose that either investment will pay 12 percent interest for 20 years and that the taxpayer is (and will remain) in the 40 percent tax bracket.

In the nonsheltered alternative, our investor must first pay 40 percent, or $800, in taxes on the $2,000, leaving just $1,200 to earn income. Then, each year, she must pay 40 percent of the interest earned to Uncle Sam before it can be reinvested. After 20 years, the total after-tax accumulation from the single $2,000 investment will be $4,820.

In the IRA alternative, the full $2,000 begins earning interest the day it enters the account. Equally important, all taxes on the interest will be deferred as it compounds. After 20 years, the $2,000 will have grown to $19,293. If our investor then withdraws the money and pays 40 percent in taxes, she will have $11,576—*more than double the sum that would have been accumulated in the equivalent taxable investment!* In fact, this example underestimates the advantage of the IRA because most retirees can time their withdrawals for years in which their tax brackets are low.

As April 15 draws near, newspapers are full of ads showing how easy it is to amass a fortune through systematic, tax-deferred savings. The ads are accurate, but misleading. It's true that $2,000 saved every year for 30 years and compounded at 12 percent interest would indeed generate a retirement nest egg of $482,665. But there's no telling how much $482,665 will buy 30 years down the road because no one knows how much inflation will have eroded the value of the dollar.

The best way to think about this question is in terms of real—that is, inflation-adjusted—interest. *Over very long periods of time, interest rates have averaged 2 to 4 percent more than the rate of inflation.* If that pattern holds in the future, the following table should give you an idea of how much your IRA nest egg would be worth:

INVEST $2,000 A YEAR FOR	IF THE INFLATION-ADJUSTED INTEREST RATE AVERAGES		
	2%	3%	4%
	YOU'LL RETIRE WITH THE EQUIVALENT OF THIS MANY OF TODAY'S DOLLARS		
10 years	$ 22,337	$ 23,616	$ 24,973
20 years	49,567	55,353	61,938
25 years	65,342	75,106	86,623
30 years	82,759	98,005	116,657
35 years	101,989	124,552	153,197
40 years	123,220	155,327	197,653

These numbers don't look quite as good as the ones in the ads. But as my grandmother never would have said, it ain't nothing to sneeze at.

There is no government limit to the number of contributions you can make to an IRA. You might, for example, choose to set aside $100 each month. The annual total, of course, can't exceed the $2,000 maximum. And all contributions must be made by April 15 of the following year— money for 1985 must be set aside by April 15, 1986, and so forth.

There is no rule against making your contribution from existing savings. The transfer from a taxable account to a tax-sheltered IRA won't increase your total savings, but it will provide a dandy tax deduction. *Nor is there a rule against borrowing to make your contribution.* Some people do this routinely, then repay the loan from their income tax refunds. It doesn't work the other way around, though: you cannot use savings in an IRA as collateral for a loan. Get caught trying it, and you will lose your tax deduction.

WHAT A DIFFERENCE A DAY MAKES

It pays to make your IRA contributions as early in the year as possible. This gives your money extra time to accumulate interest behind the tax shield. And over the years, mightier oaks from larger acorns grow.

If, for example, you invest $2,000 at 12 percent every year on January 1, you will accumulate $161,397 in 20 years. Pay, say, 40 percent income tax on the accumulated sum at the end, and you're left with $96,838. Try the experiment again, this time waiting until December 31 to make the hypothetical contribution. Now the total accumulation after 20 years will be $144,105. Subtract 40 percent tax, and you've got only $86,463.

Actually, that's not quite a fair comparison because it ignores the extra taxable interest that could be earned on the $2,000 savings from January to December each year before you make your contribution. After taxes, this comes to $6,468. Add that sum to $86,463, for a grand total of $92,931. So in this example, the net, rock-bottom benefit from contributing in January rather than December is $96,838 minus $92,931, or $3,907. Not a bad reward simply for paying attention to the calendar.

The moral: make your contribution sooner rather than later each year, and end up a little richer.

The government discourages (but doesn't prohibit) the use of IRA savings before retirement age. Unless you can prove that you have become disabled, Uncle Sam charges a 10 percent penalty tax on top of your regular income tax on withdrawals made before 59½.

By similar logic, Uncle wants you to use your IRA money, rather than leave it to your heirs. If you fail to make systematic withdrawals after the age of 70½, the Internal Revenue Service assesses a 50 percent tax on the income it thinks you should have withdrawn to support yourself.

If you happen to be a single male at age 70½, you must withdraw at least 6.67 percent of the assets in the account annually. If you are a single female, the percentage is 8.33, reflecting your longer life expectancy. If you are married, the formula is more complicated because it depends on your spouse's age as well. But don't fret. The institution that manages your IRA should be able to provide information on the minimum withdrawal schedule when you need it. And if it can't, the Internal Revenue Service can.

This institution, by the way, is called the "custodian." The government isn't very picky about who the custodian is. But you should be because it could have a big impact on how quickly your savings grow. Consider some alternatives.

Banks and Savings and Loans

These are the most popular places to set up IRAs. And for good reason. IRA deposits, like all deposits in federally insured banks, are guaranteed to $100,000. Most banks and S&Ls—for these and most other purposes, they're interchangeable—will provide custodial services for free. But watch for the fine print. They may lure you in by offering low-cost services. However, if you choose to move your IRA money to another custodian, they may whack you with a nasty penalty.

Banks typically offer savings certificates with maturities ranging from a few months to a few years. But some are willing to commit themselves to a fixed interest rate for periods as long as ten years. And some give you the option of putting IRA money in a money market account or in a variable rate CD with interest fluctuating with market conditions.

Most of what is good and bad about ordinary bank deposits applies to IRA deposits as well. Banks are free to offer any rates they please. They are free to set any interest penalty they please (above the federal minimum) on premature withdrawals. If they choose, banks can even waive the usual $1,000 minimum on money market deposits kept in an IRA account. As usual, it pays to shop around.

There are no hard-and-fast rules about which sort of account you should choose. *The shorter the term of the CD, of course, the less risk interest rates will rise and leave you behind.* Probably the most conservative strategy is to go with CDs that mature in two years or less. That way, you'll earn a bit more than you probably would with a money market deposit. But over the long haul, you would be almost certain to stay ahead of inflation. This strategy, by the way, will also give you the flexibility to move your funds to another custodian without interest penalty.

Insurance Companies

With the insurance business gradually changing into a financial planning business, insurers are pushing their regular clients to set up IRA accounts. But don't let the hard sell get to you. Some IRA savings programs available through insurance companies are pretty good, providing competitive interest rates and the option of converting the nest egg into a fixed monthly income at retirement time.

Generally, though, the disadvantages of using an insurance company as an IRA custodian far outweigh the advantages. Most plans lock you in by assessing enormous penalties for moving to another custodian. The big selling point of insurers—the ability to convert IRA cash into a guaranteed monthly check at retirement—turns out to be no advantage at all. For once you do retire, it will always be possible to "roll over" the cash from a bank or brokerage IRA into an insurance company annuity.

Still eager to do your insurance agent a favor? Buy his kid a Cabbage Patch doll or take him to lunch. Don't sign up for his IRA.

Mutual Funds

Hundreds of mutual funds with investment policies targeted toward everything from low-grade bonds to hi-tech stocks are happy to serve as IRA custodians. Most will do it without any penalty for moving the account. Many will even waive their standard minimum for initial deposits.

With certain exceptions, that makes funds a pretty good bet.

> Exception 1: *High-risk funds.*   Funds that take big risks for the purpose of making big profits may have a place in your investment portfolio. But for most people, it makes sense to think of IRAs as bedrock savings for hard times. That disqualifies funds that invest in precious metals or volatile, small capitalization stocks.
>
> Exception 2: *Tax-sheltered funds.*   IRAs are already tax-sheltered. It would thus be a waste of money to accept the lower returns to be expected on tax-exempt bond funds or tax-managed funds (see page 108).

What does that leave? At the low risk end, money market funds. Mutual funds that specialize in corporate bonds, Ginnie Maes, convertible securities, or less volatile stocks also make sense, provided you understand and accept the risks associated with interest rate changes.

Dozens of funds fit the description. See the other sections in the book for listings. *Or choose one of the families of funds listed below, all of which allow you to switch investments from one fund to another with no hassle and no cost.*

Fidelity Funds
(800) 225-6190—outside Massachusetts
(617) 523-1919

Lehman Funds
(800) 221-5350—outside New York
(212) 558-2030

Rowe Price Funds
(800) 638-5660—outside Maryland
(800) 492-1976—in Maryland

SAFECO Funds
(800) 426-6730—outside Washington State
(800) 562-6810

Scudder Funds
(800) 225-2470—outside New York
(212) 350-8370

Value Line Funds
(800) 223-0818—outside New York
(212) 687-3965

Vanguard Funds
(800) 523-7025—outside Pennsylvania
(800) 362-0530—in Pennsylvania

GILDING THE IRA INSURANCE LILY

What's safer than an IRA invested in federally insured bank deposits? An IRA also covered by "completion insurance" that guarantees some minimum benefit, should you die or become disabled.

Terms vary, but the idea is pretty much the same at the several hundred banks and S&Ls that now offer it. Say you contributed $2,000 a year until you reached age 50, then were unable to continue working. A private insurance company would continue making the payments into your account until the minimum retirement age of 59½. Some institutions offer this insurance at no charge; some charge an annual premium, which is considerably smaller than the cost of buying equivalent coverage on your own.

Other terms being equal, completion insurance is a nice bonus for conservative investors. Remember, though, other terms may not be equal. Compare the Federated Thrifty Bank, which pays an average of 11 percent on deposits with completion insurance, and the Amalgamated Profligate Bank, which pays and average of 11½ percent without completion insurance. After 30 years of $2,000 annual deposits, the account at Federated would contain $441,826. But in the same 30 years, the half percentage point more interest from Amalgamated would get you $46,770 more!

Moral: When you are investing in bank deposits for the long haul, interest rates count most. The rest is frill.

Brokers

Many brokers—discount and full-service—welcome IRA accounts. You specify how the money is to be invested, just as you would with an ordinary account. This appeals to investors who are convinced they can beat the professional money managers at their own game. But think twice before you try, too.

Most brokers charge an annual fee for IRAs, usually $50 or $100. So in the early years when the account has just a few thousand in assets, the fees could eat up a lot of the income. By the same token, a few thousand dollars is an awkward sum to invest directly in stocks or bonds. Even at a discount broker, commissions usually devour a high percentage of the total value of small stock purchases. Moreover, there is no practical way to diversify your portfolio. One could, of course, buy mutual funds through a brokerage account. But if that is all you intend to do, you might as well invest more cheaply by purchasing a "no-load" fund direct from the source.

A suggested compromise for those bent on directing their own IRAs: maintain an IRA with a bank or a no-load mutual fund until it has accumulated a minimum of $20,000. Then transfer the account to the brokerage firm of your choice. That way, you won't be eaten alive by commissions and fees.

KEOGH PLAN ACCOUNTS

Keogh plans are retirement accounts for people who work for themselves. Anyone who has self-employment income can start a Keogh. That includes people who have full-time salaried jobs but moonlight on their own. Thus, a computer programmer who worked for a chain of fast-food restaurants but did freelance consulting on the side could conceivably have a company pension plan, an IRA, and a Keogh plan!

In most respects, Keoghs work like IRAs. Contributions are deductible from taxable income. Taxes on interest and dividends earned within a Keogh are deferred until the money is withdrawn. Distributions made before age 59½ are subject to a penalty tax of 10 percent over and above the regular income tax due. You must begin to receive benefits by age 70½ or pay a penalty tax. It is illegal to use the assets of a Keogh account as security for a loan. Banks, insurance companies, mutual funds, and brokers can all serve as custodians. Contributions must be made by April 15 of the following calendar year. Virtually any sort of asset (but not collectibles, such as antiques or art) can be part of a Keogh.

There is one big difference, however. *With a Keogh, you may contribute up to 20 percent* of your self-employment income (after the deduction of business expenses) to a maximum of $30,000 a year.* And there's even a way to beat the 20 percent maximum by setting up what's called a "defined benefit" plan.

Defined benefit plans (as opposed to defined contribution plans) are intended to mimic pension plans in which the beneficiary can count on a specified amount of retirement income each month. You must set up such a plan with the advice of an actuary. Annual contributions are calculated to provide some target percentage of the contributor's working income, not to exceed $100,000 a year.

These plans can be a dandy tax shelter for self-employed people who can afford to lock away a lot of savings. But remember, they are more complicated and therefore more expensive to manage and less flexible. *Check with a good tax accountant or pension planning company before venturing further.*

Two other important considerations. Full-time employees

---

*Some, otherwise accurate, information sources say you can contribute up to 25 percent. Don't believe them. The mistake follows from misinterpretation of some particularly foggy legal jargon in the tax law.

HOW TO RETIRE A MULTIMILLIONAIRE

The big bucks may or may not buy very much when it's time to retire (see page 22). Still, it's irresistible to see just how much money Uncle Sam is willing to let you shelter in a Keogh Plan.

CONTRIBUTE THE $30,000 MAXIMUM FOR THIS LONG:	EARN THE AVERAGE OF THIS INTEREST RATE:		
	8%	10%	12%
	AND RETIRE WITH THIS MONEY IN THE BANK:		
10 years	469,365	525,935	589,638
20 years	1,482,687	1,890,075	2,420,962
30 years	3,670,376	5,428,303	8,108,778
40 years	8,393,431	14,605,554	25,774,271

who have been on your payroll for at least three years must be included in your Keogh plan. Moreover, they must receive as good a deal as you do. If, for example, you contribute 18 percent of your income, you must also contribute 18 percent of theirs.

The penalty for contributions above the maximum 20 percent allowed is equal to 6 percent of the excess. Thus, if your contribution exceeded 20 percent of your net self-employment income by $1,000, you would owe a penalty of $60. Not much, you say. But watch it: the penalty is cumulative. If, for example, you failed to withdraw the excess contribution for five years, you would owe five times $60!

PART 3
THE STRATEGIES

IS IT A GOOD INVESTMENT?

That's the right question. But there's no right answer without knowing who's doing the investing or what the investor wants to accomplish. What may be right for a 35-year-old single professional with her heart set on a time-sharing condo at Vail is almost sure to be wrong for a couple in their forties with two teenagers on the doorstep of the University of North Carolina. What's right for a 25-year-old with the dream of marketing designer frozen pizza is hardly likely to fill the bill for a 60-year-old widow with a comfortable income who wants to go to graduate school.

The investment strategies below cover a range of individuals and families with varying incomes, responsibilities, and financial goals. Find the one that fits you best, then use the TOOLS section to tailor it to your precise needs. The numbers in parentheses are page references.

ON THE WAY UP

Family status:	Single, college grad, early twenties	
Current income:	$20,000	
Income prospects:	Double within five years	
Attitude to risk:	What the heck?	
Current assets:	$5,000	
Goal:	The good life	
Recommended portfolio:	Bank NOW account (41)	$ 1,000
	Money market fund (43)	2,000
	Growth mutual fund (86)	2,000
Annual savings goals:	Individual retirement account (143)	
	—Growth mutual fund	2,000

Virtually every adult needs a checking account with unlimited checking privileges. In most cities, it's possible to find a bank that offers fee-less NOW checking with 5.25 percent interest as long as the depositor keeps $1,000 on hand. Another $2,000 belongs in a taxable money market fund, where it will earn considerably more than 5.25 percent. The remaining $2,000 could be put to work at considerably more risk in shares of one or two growth mutual funds.

Keeping $3,000 out of $5,000 in the equivalent of cash seems to be a very conservative strategy for the young investor who is willing to take chances with money. *But $3,000 is the minimum amount any investor should keep in very secure, liquid form for emergencies or unanticipated purchases.* There is no reason, though, why he or she can't start an aggressive, higher-risk investment program behind the tax shield offered by the IRA. That will also provide an immediate tax break.

Note there is no legal requirement that the entire $2,000 IRA go into a single fund or a single account. It might be interesting—or at least instructive—to try two different funds. Later on, this investor's goal may change. In which case, there should be no problem switching IRA custodians and funds. Remember, too, that IRA funds can be withdrawn in an emergency, provided you pay a small tax penalty.

AND BABY MAKES THREE

Family status:	Two-income couple, early thirties, expecting a first child
Current income:	$30,000
Income prospects:	Better than inflation
Attitude to risk:	Conservative
Current assets:	$20,000
Goals:	A house, financial security

Recommended portfolio:		
	Bank NOW account (41)	$ 1,000
	Bank money market account (42)	4,000
	Short-term bank CDs (44)	15,000

Annual savings goals:		
	Short-term bank CDs	3,000
	Individual retirement account (143)	
	—Bond mutual fund (87)	1,000
	—Balanced mutual fund (87)	1,000

The first priority here is baby and house. This family needs a riskless place to store cash, both to cover current expenses and to have the down payment on hand when the right house comes along.

Money market funds are just as liquid and virtually as safe as bank money market accounts. But many banks and savings and loans provide slightly better mortgage interest rates to established customers. So for a family about to buy a house, a bank MM account would probably offer a slight edge. Short-term (one year or less) CDs will pay a better yield than the MM account without much sacrifice of liquidity. *It probably makes sense, though, to divide the $15,000 total among several CDs.* That way, our investors could have acceses to part of the money before the CDs matured without paying an interest penalty on the entire $15,000.

This working couple is entitled to put a total of $4,000 in IRAs. *It may wish to put less, though, in order to amass cash for a down payment on a house.* This will mean paying some extra taxes. But homeowning provides the biggest tax breaks of all. So it may be worth sacrificing the taxes now to be able to buy the house sooner.

The money that does go into the IRAs might be divided between a bond fund and a balanced stock mutual fund. The bond fund should average a somewhat higher return than a bank CD. The balanced mutual fund will give our couple a chance to earn considerably more than market interest over the long term.

OZZIE AND HARRIET, 1980s STYLE

Family status:	One-income couple, mid-thirties, two young children
Current income:	$40,000
Income prospects:	Likely to grow, but no workaholics live here
Attitude to risk:	Nothing foolish
Current assets:	$30,000, plus $50,000 equity in a house
Goals:	College, financial security, money to have fun

Recommended portfolio:		
	Bank NOW account (41)	$ 2,000
	Money market account or fund (42, 43)	3,000
	Medium-term bank CDs (44)	10,000
	Balanced mutual fund (87)	5,000
	Deferred fixed annuity (112)	10,000

Annual savings goals:		
	Individual retirement account (143)	
	—Medium-term bank CDs	2,250
	Children's custodial accounts (118)	
	—Medium-term bank CDs	2,000
	Balanced mutual fund	1,000

This couple might be tempted to put extra cash in a tax-exempt money market fund. However, with two kids and mortgage interest deductions, it is very unlikely they are in a sufficiently high tax bracket to justify the lower return on a nontaxed fund.

The medium-term (say, one- to five-year) CDs should pay considerably more interest than the MM account. And there's no risk of loss should interest rates in the economy change. It pays to shop around for such CDs. The best rates are often to be had by mail from out-of-state banks. *As long as a bank or savings and loan is federally insured, it doesn't matter where it is located.*

Even investors with modest amounts of savings and conservative goals should keep some of their money in common stock mutual funds. Otherwise, they will miss any chance of higher-than-market returns.

Reminder: nonworking spouses are entitled to their own IRAs. The $2,250 maximum can be split any way you like, though $1,125 each sounds fair to me.

The earlier our investors begin to save for the kids' education, the less painful it will be later on. Interest on money in custodial accounts at a bank will be taxed at the kids' low, low rate. Banks, by the way, are usually happy to set up and maintain records for custodial accounts at no charge. *Remember, though, that money in a custodial account is the kids', not yours.* You can control its use until they are 18 (or in some states, 21). But eventually it must go to them.

AMBITION TO BURN

Family status:	Single salary earner, late twenties
Current income:	$50,000
Income prospects:	Excellent
Attitude to risk:	There's always more where that came from
Current assets:	$50,000
Goal:	Getting richer

Recommended portfolio:	Bank NOW account (41)	$ 2,000
	Money market account or fund (42, 43)	30,000
	Growth mutual fund (86)	8,000
	Deferred variable annuity (112)	
	—Growth mutual fund	10,000
Annual savings goals:	Individual retirement account (143)	
	—Growth mutual fund	2,000
	Deferred variable annuity	5,000

This affluent young investor is willing to take big risks. But the first priority for his money is a house—and a big mortgage that will generate tax deductions. That's why there is so much set aside here in a money market account or fund.

Once the house or condo is purchased, our investor can start thinking about riskier ventures. Growth mutual funds certainly qualify. Even if our investor had the time (unlikely) to play the stock market on his own, he wouldn't have accumulated enough money at this point to do it efficiently.

The deferred variable annuity also makes a lot of sense because our investor needs all the tax help he or she can get. *Any earnings in a deferred annuity will be shielded from taxes until withdrawn.* Best not to put all of one's assets behind this tax shield, though. Both the insurance company that runs the annuity program and the IRS will extract penalties for withdrawal in less than five years. If, by the way, our investor's plans change—say by marriage—he will have the option of a tax-free switch into a more conservative money market fund or bond fund without withdrawing funds from the annuity.

HOUSE RICH

Family status:	Couple, late thirties, single earner, one teenager
Current income:	$60,000
Income prospects:	Fair
Attitude to risk:	Limited
Current assets:	$100,000 equity in a house, plus $20,000
Goals:	College, financial security, minimizing taxes

Recommended portfolio:	Bank NOW account (41)	$ 2,000
	Money market account or fund (42, 43)	8,000
	Clifford trust for child (118) —Medium-term bank CDs (44)	50,000
Annual savings goals:	Individual retirement account (143) —Medium-term bank CDs	2,250

This is a well-fixed family with conservative investment goals in a high tax bracket. What makes the family's position special is that almost all its assests are concentrated in a house.

The suggested strategy is to borrow, say, $40,000 against the equity in the house, either by obtaining a bank mortgage or a "home equity loan" (the term banks now use for a second mortgage). Then put the $40,000, plus $10,000 in cash savings, into a Clifford trust in the teenager's name. *This would accomplish two goals at once: it would lower taxes and direct the family's savings toward its highest priority, the child's college expenses.*

The mortgage interest would generate a substantial tax deduction. But the interest earnings on money raised through the mortgage would be taxed at the child's low rate. The interest amassed within the trust could then be used to pay for college. Ten years after the trust is formed (and after Junior has graduated), Mom and Dad would reclaim the $50,000 principal. Then the money could be used to pay off the mortgage. Better yet, it could be reinvested conservatively to create a more diversified asset portfolio.

The suggested savings goal—two tax-sheltered IRAs totalling $2,250—seems quite modest for a family with an income of $60,000. Note, though, that the family is really saving a lot more through the vehicle of the Clifford trust.

BIG INCOME, BIG RESPONSIBILITIES

Family status:	Couple, early forties, two earners, four kids	
Current income:	$80,000	
Income prospects:	Better than inflation	
Attitude to risk:	Can't afford it	
Current assets:	$50,000 equity in a house, plus $25,000	
Goals:	College, financial security	
Recommended portfolio:	Bank superNOW account (41)	$10,000
	Intermediate-term tax-exempt fund (108)	15,000
Annual savings goals:	Children's custodial accounts (118)	
	—Medium-term bank CDs (44)	6,000
	Individual retirement account (143)	
	—Money market fund (43)	2,000
	—Ginnie Mae fund (69)	2,000
	Tax-exempt bond unit trust (106)	2,000
	Growth mutual fund (86)	2,000

A family with an income as large as $80,000 may find the greater convenience of a superNOW account, with unlimited checking privileges, worth the lower interest yield. The alternative would be to maintain an ordinary checking or NOW account, plus a money market fund or bank money market account. As usual, it pays to shop around.

The family is probably in a high tax bracket, but it has modest liquid assets. That makes an intermediate-term tax-exempt fund—one holding bonds with an average maturity of five years to ten years—a good compromise. *The after-tax yield is likely to be much higher than, say, a taxable money market fund. But the risk of loss in case of an increase in interest rates will be fairly small.*

A very high priority for this family is to save for the kids' college tuitions. The family doesn't have enough accumulated savings to make a Clifford trust worthwhile. But it would make sense to make regular gifts to custodial accounts in the children's names. That would save a lot on taxes because all interest earnings would be taxed at the kids' lower rates. It's worth remembering, though, that the money in custodial accounts belongs to the kids, not the parents. When college time rolls around and little Julian decides to head for Nepal rather than Berkeley, that's his business.

The next priority for this family is balanced savings for the long haul, preferably in ways that minimize taxes. The IRAs, split between money market savings and higher-yield Ginnie Maes, would be a very conservative beginning. *Long-term tax-exempt bond unit trusts are a good bet for high after-tax yield.* A modest commitment to growth mutual funds would make sense for the only unsheltered savings dollars.

BUSINESS FIRST

Family status:	Childless couple, early thirties, self-employed
Current income:	$40,000
Income prospects:	Great—if the business succeeds
Attitude to risk:	High risks acceptable for high gain
Current assets:	Illiquid investment in the business, plus $20,000
Goals:	No boss, the good life

Recommended portfolio:	Bank NOW account (41)	$ 2,000
	Bank money market account (42)	8,000
	Short-term bank CDs (44)	10,000
Annual savings goals:	Short-term bank CDs	3,000
	Individual retirement account (143)	
	—Short-term bank CDs	4,000

One of the classic errors made by people starting new businesses is to underestimate their cash needs. *That's why this couple would be wise to keep all its nonbusiness assets in very liquid form.*

It usually makes sense for most investors to choose the federally insured bank or savings and loan that offers the highest interest rates. But this couple is special. To begin with, it doesn't have very much in liquid savings, so a percentage point more or less won't make much difference to the bottom line. What could matter a lot more is the establishment of a good relationship with a single bank—a bank, for example, that is likely to lend money to cover a temporary shortfall, a bank that would be inclined to honor deposited checks as cash for their steady customers.

It would be no great tragedy if this young, childless couple delayed the creation of a retirement savings plan. Still, the potential tax savings make IRAs virtually irresistible, even for the liquidity-hungry.

Money in an IRA is less liquid than unsheltered bank savings. *But in a pinch, the IRA money could be withdrawn at the price of paying a modest tax penalty.* In any case, such an emergency withdrawal would probably not be necessary. While it is not legal for a bank to lend money using the assets of an IRA as collateral, many business-oriented banks informally consider IRA deposits as another reason to lend money to a loyal customer.

HANDS-ON MONEY MANAGEMENT

Family status:	Two-income couple, late thirties, one child	
Current income:	$50,000	
Income prospects:	Better than inflation	
Attitude to risk:	Will listen to reason	
Current assets:	$30,000 equity in a house, plus $40,000	
Goals:	College, control of own finances	
Recommended portfolio:	Bank NOW account (41)	$ 2,000
	Money market account or fund (42, 43)	3,000
	Medium-term bank CDs (44)	15,000
	Common stocks, bonds, convertibles (73)	20,000
	Clifford trust for child (118) —Loan to parents	20,000
Annual savings goals:	Individual retirement account (143) —Mutual fund with switching privileges (149)	4,000
	Addition to stocks and bonds (73)	2,000

This couple wants to buy securities on its own rather than trusting its financial fate to mutual funds or banks. But it must also plan for a child's education. The strategy suggested here offers a way to maximize financial control and generate the necessary savings for college. Yet it is also a strategy that will help minimize tax liability.

The couple invests $20,000 in stocks, bonds, and convertibles. Next it sets up a Clifford trust for the child with the remaining $20,000. Then it borrows back the $20,000 at market interest rates, investing the proceeds in bank savings.

The interest paid into the trust is a tax-deductible expense for the parents. The interest income earned by the trust is taxable at the child's low tax rate, producing a net tax savings for the family. Note that the Clifford trust must be set up in such a way as to permit the loan to the parents. *In fact, as with any Clifford trust, the arrangement must be carefully checked by a lawyer before it is locked into place.*

The money in our couple's IRAs could also be invested directly in stocks and bonds. But with small sums available in the newly formed IRA accounts, the expenses of self-direction would be extremely high. Hence the suggested compromise, putting the IRA money in a family of mutual funds that permit an investor to switch from a money market fund to a bond fund to a conservative stock fund to a growth stock fund, and so forth. *Once the sums in the IRAs grow to reasonable size, it will always be possible to move the money into a self-directed IRA at a brokerage firm.*

REFURBISHING THE EMPTY NEST

Family status:	Couple, late forties, one salary earner, kids grown up
Current income:	$30,000
Income prospects:	Stable
Attitude to risk:	Very limited
Current assets:	$60,000 equity in a house, plus $10,000
Goals:	Financial security, extra income for retirement

Recommended portfolio:	Bank NOW account (41)	$ 2,000
	Money market account (42)	3,000
	Deferred fixed annuity (112)	5,000
Annual savings goals:	Individual retirement account (143) —Medium-term bank CDs (44)	2,250
	U.S. Savings Bonds (115)	1,000
	Balanced mutual fund (87)	1,000

In the past, this family used most of its savings to educate the kids and reduce the amount owed on their home mortgage. Now it's time to start building a savings base that will permit a comfy retirement.

It's almost always sensible to keep $5,000 in very liquid form; hence the wisdom of supplementing the cash in a NOW account with money in a higher-interest money market account. The remaining $5,000, which hopefully won't be touched for two decades or more, can be put away in a secure, high-yielding deferred annuity.

IRAs should be the first priority for ongoing savings. A couple with just $10,000 in basic savings would most sensibly stick with very conservative securities—here the highest-yielding, federally insured bank CDs they can find. By the same token, *U.S. Savings Bonds would make a good buy: they're riskless, generate competitive interest yields, and defer taxes*. For maximum flexibility, U.S. Savings Bonds should be purchased in small denominations.

Balanced mutual funds are not riskless. But they would give this couple a chance for substantially greater earnings over the long pull.

Family status:	Working couple, late fifties, kids grown up	
Current income:	$80,000	
Income prospects:	Stable	
Attitude to risk:	Moderate	
Current assets:	$75,000 equity in a house, plus $20,000	
Goal:	Maintaining high living standard in retirement	
Recommended portfolio:	Bank superNOW account (41)	$ 5,000
	Deferred fixed annuity (112)	10,000
	Tax-exempt bond fund (108)	5,000
Annual savings goals:	Individual retirement account (143)	
	—Junk bond funds (60)	4,000
	Deferred variable annuity (114)	
	—In growth funds (115)	5,000
	Tax-exempt bond unit trust (106)	10,000

Like a lot of people with good incomes, this couple has not saved much outside its home equity. A decade of substantial savings would go a long way toward righting the balance and preventing a sharp drop in living standards at retirement.

The superNOW account is a convenience, not an investing necessity. The unlimited checking privilege makes it possible to consolidate all liquid assets in a single account.

This couple is in a high tax bracket. That's why all the suggested investments are, one way or another, "tax-advantaged." Income from the deferred annuities isn't taxed until it's withdrawn—in this case, presumably, after the couple has retired and is in a lower tax bracket. Current income on the tax-exempt bond fund and unit trusts is free of federal taxes. *People in high-tax states—such as New York, Pennsylvania, and California—should also look for funds and trusts that are free of state and local taxes.*

Junk bonds aren't necessarily junky. They're just a little riskier than so-called "investment-grade" bonds and thus pay higher yields. A junk bond fund would make a solid investment for an IRA.

Deferred variable annuities allow money to accumulate in a growth mutual fund without current tax liability. Since this couple has a greater need for accumulation than liquidity, the deferred variable annuity makes a lot of sense.

STARTING OVER—WITH HELP

Family status:	Recently divorced salary earner, mid-forties, without dependents
Current income:	$12,000
Income prospects:	Uncertain
Attitude to risk:	Very conservative
Current assets:	$100,000 equity in a house, plus $200,000
Goals:	Financial security, personal earning capacity

Recommended portfolio:	Bank NOW account (41)	$ 2,000
	Money market account or fund (42, 43)	3,000
	Medium-term bank CDs (44)	100,000
	Deferred fixed annuity (112)	50,000
	Ginnie Mae fund (71)	20,000
	Balanced mutual fund (87)	25,000
Annual savings goals:	No current net savings, but transfer $2,000 a year to IRA (143)	

This recently divorced investor finds herself with substantial assets but relatively little earning power. Her goal is to invest the assets from her separation settlement to ensure a decent living standard while she gets on with the job of becoming financially independent.

The medium-term bank CDs will provide secure, current income of $10,000 or so. They could also be a source of liquidity on which to draw should she decide to go back to school to retrain for the job market. The smaller sums in Ginnie Maes and balanced mutual funds are somewhat riskier investments but should offer higher expected returns.

It probably also makes sense for our investor to put away $50,000 in a deferred fixed annuity. The money would be accessible without penalty in ten years should she need it to live on. And it's a nice, set-it-and-forget-it investment on which to base retirement.

It would be unrealistic to expect our investor to save from current income. *But as long as she is employed and must pay taxes, she ought to take advantage of the tax break by transferring $2,000 a year into an IRA.* The IRA money could be conservatively invested in bank CDs.

EASING INTO RETIREMENT

Family status:	Two-income couple, late fifties, with no dependents
Current income:	$30,000
Income prospects:	On the decline
Attitude to risk:	Conservative
Current assets:	$75,000 equity in a house, plus $50,000, plus vested pension rights
Goal:	Comfortable retirement

Recommended portfolio:		
	Bank NOW account (41)	$ 2,000
	Money market account or fund (42, 43)	3,000
	Medium-term bank CDs (44)	20,000
	Balanced mutual fund (87)	10,000
	Deferred fixed annuity (112)	15,000

Annual savings goals:		
	Individual retirement account (143)	
	—Ginnie Mae fund (71)	2,000
	—Balanced mutual fund	2,000

This is a classic position for a middle-income couple poised for retirement. It would do well to avoid the classic errors. First, our couple should not buy tax-exempt bonds because it is not in a high enough tax bracket to justify the lower pretax return. *Second, our couple should resist the temptation to invest a large proportion of its savings in long-term, fixed income securities.* Long-term securities would provide more current income. But such an unbalanced portfolio would make our couple extremely vulnerable to inflation.

The wiser course would be a lower-yield but virtually inflation-proof mix of medium-term fixed income securities, such as bank CDs, plus a deferred annuity whose value doesn't change with variation in interest rates. The mutual funds are riskier. But the risk must be balanced against the opportunity for appreciation.

Investors under 70 should continue to put money into IRAs as long as they are working and paying taxes—if necessary transferring savings from other investments. A high-yielding Ginnie Mae bond fund wouldn't be a bad place to put the cash, especially if the fixed-yield investment is balanced with purchases of mutual fund shares.

SECURING THE GOOD LIFE

Family status:	Two-income couple, mid-forties, with one teenage child	
Current income:	$150,000	
Income prospects:	Still growing	
Attitude to risk:	Why take chances?	
Current assets:	$150,000 equity in a house, plus $500,000	
Goals:	Living well, financial security	
Recommended portfolio:	Bank superNOW account (41)	$ 10,000
	Tax-exempt money market fund (50)	15,000
	Clifford trust for child (118)	
	—Treasury strips (65)	50,000
	—Taxable money market fund (43)	25,000
	Tax-exempt bond unit trust (106)	200,000
	Aggressive growth mutual fund (86)	50,000
	Precious metals (123)	25,000
	International mutual fund (87)	25,000
	Deferred fixed annuity (112)	50,000
	Deferred variable annuity (114)	
	—Growth mutual fund	50,000
Annual savings goals:	Individual retirement account (143)	
	—Medium-term CDs (44)	4,000
	Tax-exempt bond unit trust (106)	10,000
	Balanced mutual fund (87)	5,000

Most people would like to have this family's "problem"—namely, how to manage very substantial assets. The suggested strategy here is conservative, stressing preservation of capital and minimization of taxes in a variety of possible futures.

The Clifford trust would allow this family to set aside assets for college while paying taxes at its child's much lower rate.

Since the family is almost certainly in a high tax bracket, it is among the select few that can benefit from using a tax-exempt money market fund to store spare cash.

The largest single investment in the suggested portfolio is tax-exempt bond unit trusts. Given an opportunity, virtually any bond salesperson or broker would try to steer this family toward individual issues of bonds rather than unit trusts. It's true that bonds would generate slightly higher yield. However, if this family is typical, it doesn't have the time or expertise to judge their quality. *The family would probably be better to stick with unit trusts, taking care to mix a number of medium- and long-term trusts so that the average maturity of the underlying bonds is about ten years.*

Other recommended purchases include international mutual funds and precious metals. Both are rainy day investments, likely to rise sharply in value when domestic common stocks and bonds are falling.

Note, too, that $100,000 is divided between fixed and variable deferred annuities. Fixed annuities are out of fashion; variable annuities were never in fashion. But carefully chosen, both offer excellent tax shelters for high-income investors seeking diversified portfolios.

RETIREMENT PLUS

Family status:	Retired couple, late sixties, with no dependents
Current income:	$35,000 (pensions, social security, and interest)
Income prospects:	Fixed
Attitude to risk:	Very conservative
Current assets:	$100,000 equity in a house, plus $100,000
Goals:	Security, comfort, travel

Recommended portfolio:		
	Bank NOW account (41)	$ 2,000
	Money market account or fund (42, 43)	8,000
	Medium-term bank CDs (44)	40,000
	Ginnie Mae pass thru security (69)	25,000
	Balanced mutual fund (87)	25,000

Annual savings goals:	No net savings, but the maximum IRA contribution if the couple is still working part time and if both people are under age 70

The highest priority for this middle-income retired couple is preservation of purchasing power. The bank CDs and money market assets are invulnerable to changes in interest rates. The same can't be said for the Ginnie Mae pass-thru security. But the high current income is solid compensation. *Anyone who buys a Ginnie Mae should take care to avoid securities selling above par.* See page 70 for the explanation.

Balanced mutual funds offer a chance for capital appreciation, as well as a higher expected total return than the lower risk securities in the portfolio. It would probably pay to buy shares in two or three different funds.

It's worth remembering, too, that income from part-time work can be shunted into an IRA, reducing tax liability. Such IRA contributions need not be true savings; it's perfectly legal to transfer the money from other savings.

A last thought: a lot of this couple's assets are locked up in equity in a house. Our couple may wish to sell it, buy a smaller house or condo, and conservatively invest the resulting cash. Alternatively, it could rent rather than buy. People over age 55 have a single opportunity to take up to a $125,000 capital gain on the sale of a house without incurring any tax liability.

A WELL-PADDED RETIREMENT

Family status:	Single retiree, late sixties, with no dependents
Current income:	$50,000 (pensions, social security, and interest)
Income prospects:	Fixed
Attitude to risk:	Conservative
Current assets:	$150,000 equity in a house, plus $250,000
Goals:	Security, comfort, travel

Recommended portfolio:		
Bank NOW account (41)		$ 5,000
Tax-exempt money market fund (50)		20,000
Ginnie Mae fund (71)		25,000
Balanced mutual fund (87)		50,000
Deferred fixed annuity (114)		50,000
Tax-exempt put bonds or put bond unit trust (106)		50,000
Tax-exempt bond unit trust (106)		50,000

Annual savings goals:	Deferred fixed annuity	5,000

The portfolio for this affluent retiree is geared to high current income, tax avoidance, preservation of capital, and simplicity of management.

This retiree's taxable income is probably high enough to warrant the use of a low-yield tax-exempt money market fund for a portion of liquid assets. *But tax-exempt put bonds (or put bond unit trusts) would probably pay a considerably higher yield*. They are a good compromise between the higher liquidity of a money market fund and the higher yield of longer-term, interest sensitive securities.

Investors who want the simplicity of a steady flow of cash can usually arrange to receive a fixed monthly check from their mutual funds. The check, of course, may represent more or less than the investors' monthly income. The difference comes in the form of automatic purchases or liquidations of shares in the fund.

Why might retired investors continue to save money? To offset the slow decline in purchasing power of their assets caused by inflation. See page 22.

AFTERWORD

KEEPING UP

Unless investing is your profession (or hobby), there's little point to combing three newspapers a day for financial tips or to devoting hours each morning to business reports on radio or TV. Most people, most of the time, are better off creating investment strategies to fit their needs, then sticking by them.

That doesn't mean, though, that total ignorance is bliss. A few hours spent each month keeping up with changes in the world of personal finance can pay off handsomely. Hence this abbreviated guide to where to find reliable information at minimum of time, cost, and hype.

The Wall Street Journal. America's premier business publication. No other source comes close in providing up-to-date reporting on events in the world of business and economics. And it has recently beefed up its coverage of personal finance, devoting roughly a column a day to the subject under the heading "Your Money Matters." But there's more in the *Journal* than you may need or want to know on a daily basis. Read it regularly to be an informed citizen. Or consider buying it from the newsstands when big events that affect your own finances—e.g., tax reform, changes in banking laws—are in the news.

The New York Times. Sunday business section. Good feature stories related to personal finance, plus summaries of weekly activity in the stock, bond, and options markets. One of the nicest features is that it is full of ads for bank CDs, unit trusts, discount brokers, mutual funds, new investment products, and so forth.

Barron's. A weekly tabloid full of well-researched gossip, investigative reporting, and "insider" stories about Wall Street. Almost every issue also contains a short primer on some aspect of business or finance—the money supply figures, stock index futures, or the like. The tables in the back are the most complete summary of stock, bond, and options transactions available to the public. In general, though, *Barron's* is aimed at professionals; there are slim pickings here for all but the most dedicated investors.

Business Week. *BW* is to business news what *Time* is to general news. It's broad, crisply written, and up-to-date. Weekly issues have a "Personal Business Supplement," which covers trends in personal investing. Of most interest to individual investors is the year-end "Investment Outlook" issue that provides a good market-by-market summary of where it may pay to put your money.

Forbes. Smart, irreverent stories about business and investing. A painless, entertaining way to keep up with the latest on taxes, stock market analysis, mutual funds, and new investment products. If you want to subscribe to a single publication that covers both business news and personal investing, *Forbes* is probably the magazine of choice.

Fortune. Similar to *Forbes* in content, approach, and frequency of publication (every other week), but not as cleverly written. The personal investing column at the back is often smart and insightful.

Money. The largest circulation monthly devoted exclusively to personal finance. Unlike *Forbes* or *Barron's*, it assumes subscribers have little prior knowledge of business or economics—and not much interest in them beyond the ways they affect personal money matters. Readers familiar with the contents of this book may find it a bit repetitive. Like all Time-Life publications, though, it is carefully researched and edited for readability.

Personal Investor. An easy-to-read monthly not far in spirit from *Money.* One big difference: it covers only investing. There are no stories on how to survive a tax audit or get the best deal on a video recorder. But the investment news and advice are first-rate.

Fact. A relatively new monthly personal finance magazine, published by the company that puts out the Value Line Investment Survey and runs the Value Line group of mutual funds. Aimed at more adventurous investors than *Money,* it covers more esoteric subjects. An excellent source of information about investing in stamps, coins, art, and other collectibles.

Sylvia Porter's Personal Finance Magazine. A "down-scale" version of *Money,* geared to lower-income savers and savers just starting out. Readers of this book will already know most of what's in it.

Financial World. A monthly magazine concentrating on news about the stock market. Lots of stories about which broker is hot, which electric utility might go bust, which personal computer software works best for analyzing stocks, and so forth. Roughly half of each issue consists of a pullout section listing basic data on 3,000 stocks. *Financial World* is too specialized for casual investors but may be a help for investors who want to try their hands at picking individual stocks.

American Association of Individual Investors Journal. Solid, no-nonsense advice on how to pick a broker, mutual fund, tax shelter, and so forth—sort of a *Consumer Reports* for small investors. Membership in the association ($44 a year) gets you the journal, plus discounts on subscriptions to most business magazines. Write AAII, 612 North Michigan Ave., Chicago, Illinois 60611.

J. K. Lasser's Your Income Tax. (Simon and Schuster). There is a ton of competition. But this fat, yellow paperback is the most authoritative annual guide to the personal income tax available. A must for investors who want to know how to keep up with changes in laws about retirement plans, sales of securities, gifts to minors, and so forth.

The Mutual Fund Letter.   A monthly providing lots of information on the investment policies and records of individual mutual funds, plus recommendations. Not cheap ($60 annually). But may be worth it if you want to invest substantial amounts in mutual funds. Write Investment Information Services, 205 West Wacker Drive, Chicago, Illinois 60606.

The Value Line Investment Survey.   The single most complete guide to the stock market. Some subscribers simply use it as a reference source; each weekly loose-leaf issue provides data for some 1,700 stocks. Most subscribers simply take its advice in picking individual stocks. Value Line occasionally stumbles. But, on average, its picks beat the market. Available by subscription only (and at considerable cost). Call (800) 331-1750 for the current price.

INDEX

AARP U.S. Government Money Trust, 49, 49 n
Abusive tax shelters, 14
Account executives, 17
Agency bonds, 57–59
Amalgamated Bank of New York, 53
American Association of Individual Investors (AAII), 89; *Journal*, 191
American Bond Exchange, 59, 135
American Stock Exchange, 75, 77; Market Index, 77
American Investors Income Fund, 61
Analytic Optioned Equity Fund, 142
Annual Fees: IRAs, 151; no-load funds, 64, 108–109
Annuities, 112–114, 148
Anschutz, Philip, 26
Archimedes, 5
Asian Development Bank, 58
Asset management accounts, 83–84
Assets (liquid): and inflation, 187; modest, 169; and new businesses, 171; substantial, 179
AT&T bonds, 55, 60
Australia, 123, 126, 129
Austrian gold coins, 126, 131

Babson Income Trust, 64
Back-end load funds, 86
Balanced mutual funds, 87, 91; in personalized portfolios, 160–62, 174–75, 178, 182–87
Baldwin-United Corporation, 113–114
Bank for Co-ops bonds, 57
Bank Certificates of Deposit (CDs). See Certificates of Deposit
Bank money market accounts. See Money market accounts
Bank NOW accounts. See NOW accounts
Banks, 3, 17, 44, 57–58, 69, 105, 128; checking accounts in, 40–42; and compound interest, 20–21; deregulation of interest rates and, 45, 47; and IRAs, 147–48, 150–51; and mortgages, 25, 68–69; new business and, 171; savings accounts in, 39–40, 46, 116
Bank SUPERNOW accounts. See SUPERNOW accounts
Barclays Asset Management Account, 84

Barron's, 17, 87, 95, 190
Bearer bonds, 97
Bell Telephone bonds, 55, 60
Beneficial National Bank, 53
Beta coefficient, 88–89
Bevill, Bresler and Schulman, 82
Bid and asked price, 57–58; and Ginnie Mae listings, 70–71
Bond exchanges, 59, 67, 135
Bond Investors Guarantee (BIG), 101
Bond mutual funds, 63–65; in personalized portfolios, 160–61, 165. See also Tax-exempt bond funds
Bond unit trusts, 62–64. See also Tax-exempt unit trusts
Bonds, 28, 55–72, 135–36. See also Tax-exempt bonds
"Brand-name" tax-exempt bonds, 105
Brokerage firms. See Discount brokers; Full service brokers; Stockbrokers
Bullion, 125–34
Business Week, 87, 190
Butterfield Savings Association, 53

California, 44, 45, 57, 110, 114, 177
California Tax-Free Money Fund, 50
Callahan Mining, 133
Call provisions, 62, 67–68, 79, 97, 100, 105, 107
Calls, 138–42; "covered," 141
Canada, 123, 126, 129, 131
Canadian Maple Leaf coin, 126–28, 131
Capital appreciation, 86–87, 125, 136–37, 185
Capital gains, 87, 119, 141; and sale of house, 121, 185; and tax swaps, 103–104
Capital Preservation Fund, 48
Capital preservation, 55, 125
Cash value life insurance, 18–19
CATS (Certificates of Accrual on Treasury Securities), 67
Certificates of Deposit (CDs), 3, 25, 44–48, 55; banks issuing, 53–54; and IRAs, 147–48; in personalized portfolios, 160–63, 166, 168, 174–75, 178–79, 181; with variable rates, 46, 147
Charles Schwab, 82
Chartism, 30–31

Checking accounts, 40–41, 46–47
Checkwriting privilege, 40–43, 46, 49–50, 83, 108, 169
Children: and college tuition, 118–119, 167, 169, 173, 183; first baby portfolio, 160–61; and income transfers, 117–21
Churning, 4–5
Citibank Focus management account, 84
Citibank of New York, 119–21, 128–29
Citibank Precious Metals Service, 129
Clifford trusts, 68, 118–119; in personalized portfolios, 166–67, 169, 172–73, 182–83
Closed-end funds, 85, 93–95
CMOs (collateralized mortgage obligation), 72
Coins, gold, 125–28
Collateralized bonds, 59, 102, 105
Collaterized mortgage obligation (CMO), 72
Collateralized pass thru securities, 68
College tuition, 66, 117–21
Colonial Savings Bank, 53
Columbia Fixed Income Security Fund, 64
Commissions (brokerage), 4, 8; closed-end funds, 94; covered options, 142–43; discount brokers and, 87; gold/silver certificates, 128, 133–34; syndicated investments, 12; tax-exempts, 100, 106; tax swaps, 104; Treasury bonds, 57; unit trusts, 63, 107–108
Commodities market, 7–8
Common stock mutual funds, 84–95; closed-end, 93–95; for IRAs, 148–50; objectives of, 86–87; performance, 29, 90–93, 95; ratings, 87–90; selected list, 90–95; and variable annuities, 114–115
Common stocks, 3–7, 73–90; compared to bonds, 27–28; buying tips, 80; and covered options, 138–42; research and information, 12–13, 16, 29–31, 189–92. See also Common stock mutual funds; Convertible securities; Preferred stocks; Stockbrokers
Compound interest, 20–23, 45, 65
Congress, 9, 14, 24, 73, 143–44
See also United States
Continental Savings Association, 52
"Conversion value," 136
Convertible-term CDs, 45–46
Convertible securities, 135–38, 149
Corporate bonds, 59–60, 79, 97, 149; call and put provisions, 62; listings, 60–61; mutual funds, 63–65; unit trusts, 62–63; zero coupon, 66–68
See also Junk bonds
Couples, investment strategies.
See Investment strategies, couples
Coupon rate, 56–57; and tax swaps, 104
Covered options, 138–42
Credit card financing, 7
Credit cards, 39, 41, 83–84
Credit ratings, of bonds, 59, 101–102

Credit unions, 39–40
Crest Savings Bank, 53
Crown loan, 118
Custodial accounts: for children, 118, 163, 169. See also IRAs
Custodian, 147–48

Daily Cash Accumulation, 49
Daily sales volume, 60
Deak-Perera, 128, 134
Deferred fixed annuities, 112–114; in personalized portfolios, 162, 174–75, 177, 183, 187
Deferred variable annuities, 114–115; in personalized portfolios, 165, 177, 183
Defined benefit plan, 152–53
Depreciation allowance, 9–10, 121–22
Diamonds, 124
Discount brokers, 17, 80–83, 151
Discount Brokerage, 83
Discounted investments: CDs, 45; diversified closed-end funds, 94–95; T-bills, 44, 65; zero coupon bonds, 65
Diversification, 25–29, 80; in call options, 142; and corporate bonds, 62–63; and gold stock funds, 130; and limited partnerships, 14–15; mutual funds and, 85, 87, 89, 95; and precious metals, 123; and unit trusts, 107
Dividends, 75, 79
Divorce settlements, 105, 178–79
Dodge, Mrs. Horace, 8–9, 11
Dow-Jones Industrial Average (DJIA), 76
Down market performance of mutual funds, 86, 89–95, 142
Down payments, 6, 122, 161
Dreyfus A Bond Plus, 64
Dreyfus Group Funds, 51
Dreyfus Money Market Instruments, 48
Dreyfus Tax-Exempt Money Market Fund, 50

Effective annual yield, 21, 45, 53
Efficient market hypothesis, 29–31
E. F. Hutton, 129
Emergency funds, 159, 171
Empire Tax-Free Money Market, 50
Equity in real estate, 167, 175, 177, 185
Equity stock ownership, 73
Expandable CDs, 45
Expected return, 26–27
Exxon, 59

Fact, 17, 87, 191
Fannie Mae securities, 72
Farmers Home Administration, 58
Federal Deposit Insurance Corporation (FDIC), 44
Federal Farm Credit, 58
Federal Home Loan Banks, 58
Federal Home Loan Mortgage Corporation, 50, 71–72
Federal Housing Administration, 58
Federal Land Bank, 57

Federal National Mortgage Association, 58, 72
Federal Reserve, 7, 39, 44, 53
Federal Savings and Loan Insurance Corporation (FSLIC), 44
Federal Trade Commission (FTC), 19
Fidelity Group Funds, 51, 64, 149
Fidelity High Income Fund, 61
Fidelity Source, 82
Fidelity USA, 84
Financial Bond Shares, 64
Financial Guaranty Insurance Corporation (FGIC), 101
Financial World, 191
First Savings Association, 54
First Variable Rate Fund for Government Income, 48
Fixed income investments, 55–72, 111; cf. convertibles, 135–36; deferred annuities, 112–115
Fixed rate mortgages, 25
Floating rate bonds, 102, 106
Forbes, 29, 86–87, 94, 190
Ford, Henry, 29
Ford Credit, 60
Foreign stocks, 29, 87, 92–93
Fortune, 190
Franklin Group Money Funds, 49
Franklin Savings Association, 54
Freddie Mac Participation Certificates (PCs), 71–72
FSLIC, 44
Full-service brokerage houses, 16–17, 128

Gateway Option Income Fund, 142
Gemstones, 124
General obligation bonds, 100, 102, 105
General partners, 12–13
Getty, John Paul, 26
Gifts, 117–119; of housing to family members, 121–22.
  See also College tuition
Gill Savings Association, 52
Ginnie Maes (GNMAs), 69–71, 149; in personalized portfolios, 169, 179, 181, 184, 186; unit trusts, 71
GIT Investment Funds, 52, 52n
GMAC, 60
GNMAs. *See* Ginnie Maes
Golconda Investors, 129
Gold bullion and certificates, 5, 123–29, 131–32, 134
Gold funds, 95, 129–31
Government-backed securities.
  See Agency bonds; International bonds; T-bills; U.S. Savings Bonds; U.S. Treasury bonds
Growth mutual funds, 86–87, 90–91; in personalized portfolios, 159, 165, 169, 177
Guam, 103, 110

Haas Securities
Hecla Mining Company, 133

Hedge securities, 135–42
Hedging strategies, 29, 111, 135
Hidden-load funds, 86
Home ownership, 23–25, 160–61; equity in, 175, 177, 185; equity loan, 167; sale of, 23–24, 185
Housing gifts, 121–22. *See also* Home ownership
Hungarian 100 Corona, 126
Hunt, H. L. and family, 26, 132

IBM, 16, 59
Implicit rent, 24
Income, 23–24; and retirement accounts, 143–44, 146, 152; transfers, 118. *See also* Tax brackets and income
Income mutual funds, 87, 91–92
Income taxes, 3, 8–15, 22, 42, 57, 87; on corporate and Treasury zeros, 66–67; covered call writing and, 141. *See also* State and local governments, taxes; Tax brackets and income; Tax-exempt bonds; Tax shelters; Withdrawal penalties
Income tax tables, 98–99
"Individual Investor's Guide to No-Load Mutual Funds," 89
Individual Retirement Accounts.
  See IRAs
Inflation: long-term fixed-income securities and, 181; precious metals and, 124–25, 132, 134; effect on purchasing power, 22–23, 66, 145; and short-term CDs, 148; tax-exempt zeros and, 68
Inflation-adjusted interest.
  See Real interest
Ingot coins, 125–27, 132
Insurance, 17–19; for IRAs, 150; on tax-exempts, 101
Insurance companies, 17–19, 60, 66, 69, 148; and annuities, 113–115, 165
Inter-American Development Bank, 58
Interest rates, 3, 5, 39; average over inflation, 145; on bank accounts, 40–42, 46; and bonds, 28, 55–62, 102–106, 116–117, 177; and call provisions, 97, 100; CDs and, 44–46, 48, 163; and convertibles, 136; on deferred annuities, 112–113; and gold prices, 124–25; and IRAs, 146–51; money market accounts and funds, 42–44; 1986 deregulation of, 39–42, 45, 47; on pass thru securities, 69–72; on permanent life insurance savings, 19; on stocks, 75; on T-bills, 44; on zero coupon bonds, 65–67, 105. *See also* Compound interest; Mortgages
Intermediate-term tax-exempts, 111, 168–69
Internal Revenue Service (IRS), 8, 44, 85, 104, 114; IRA withdrawals and, 147; tax shelters and 14–15
International bonds, 58–59
International mutual funds, 87, 92–93; in personalized portfolio, 183

"In the money" calls, 139–40
"Investment value" (convertible bonds), 136
Investment strategies:
    for married couples, 160–63, 166–77, 182–83
    and retirement, 180–81, 184–87
    for singles, 158–59, 164–65, 178–79
International Telephone and Telegraph, 138–41
IRAs, 67–68, 152; used as collateral, 171; "completion insurance" and, 150; contributions, 145–46, 163, 185; custodians, 147–51; limits, 143–45; mutual funds for, 149–50; withdrawal penalties. See also Investment strategies
IRS. See Internal Revenue Service

J. K. Lasser's Your Income Tax, 191–92
John Hancock Cash Management Trust, 50
Junk bonds, 60–61

Kemper Money Market Fund, 51
Keogh retirement accounts, 67–68, 151–53, 152 n
Keystone Custodian Funds B-4, 61
Kiplinger, 17
Korea Fund, 95

Lehman Fund, 149
Leverage, 5–8, 10, 130, 140
Lexington Gold Fund, 129
Lexington GNMA Fund, 71
Lexington Tax-Free Daily Income Fund, 51
Liberty Funds, 61, 65
Liebling, A. J., 88
Life insurance, 17–19
Limited partnerships, 12–15
Liquid investments, 39–54
Liquidity: Agency bonds, 58; bond funds, 64, 108; bond unit trusts, 63; corporate bonds, 59–60; junk bonds, 61; and mutual funds, 85; new businesses and, 171; pass thru securities, 69, 71–72; precious metals, 124, 126–27, 130, 132–34; stocks and exchanges, 75; tax exempts, 103, 105, 106; Treasury strips, 67; U.S. Savings Bonds, 116
Load funds, 85–86
Loads. See Sales charges
Loans: Clifford trust and, 119; to dependents, 118; and home equity, 167
Long-term CDs, 44–45
Long-term securities, 55–56, 60–61, 103, 169, 181. See also Bonds; Tax-exempt bonds; U.S. Treasury bonds
Long-term tax-exempt bond funds, 111
Long-term tax-exempt unit trusts, 169
Low-load funds, 86
Ludwig, Daniel K., 26

Malkiel, Burton, 22 n
Management, of investments, 29, 85, 90

Margin sales, 7
Marquette de Bary, 82
Mars, Forrest E., 26
Massachusetts, 44
Maturity dates: of T-bills, 43–44; and tax swaps, 104; of Treasury bonds, 56–57, 61; and unit trusts, 107–108
MBS (mortgage-backed security), 72
Medallions, 125–26
Medium-term bank CDs, 162–63, 166, 168, 174, 178–79, 181
Merrill Lynch, 129
Mexico, 123; coins, 126–28, 131
Minnesota, 44
Money, 17, 190
Money market accounts, 3, 25, 42–43, 47–48, 84, 147–48; in personalized portfolios, 163, 169, 171, 175, 178; list of, 52
Money market funds, 43, 47–51, 54; in personalized portfolios, 165, 159, 172, 178, 180; tax-exempt, 50–51, 163, 183, 187
Money Market Management Trust, 50
Moody's, 59, 101
Mortgage-backed securities (MBS), 68–72
Mortgages, 10; parents/students housing and, 121–22; pass thru securities, 68–72; rates, 25; second, 167
Municipal Bond Insurance Corporation (MBIA), 101
Municipal bonds, 8–9, 11.
    See also Tax-exempt bonds
Muriel Siebert, 83
Mutual Fund Letter, 192
Mutual funds, 5, 13, 31; and diversification, 28–29; in Ginnie Maes, 71; in gold, 129; for IRAs, 149–50; in junk bonds, 61; no-load, 16, 71, 89, 151; and options, 142. See also Bond mutual funds; Common stock mutual funds; Money market funds; Tax-exempt bond funds

NASDAQ (National Association of Securities Dealers Automated Quotations) National Market Index, 77
National Credit Union Administration (NCUA), 40
Neuberger and Berman Government Money Fund, 48
Newsletters, 5
New York (State), 44, 57, 103, 110, 114, 177
New York Bond Exchange, 59, 67, 135
"New York close" price, 138
New York stock exchange, 75; Common Stock Index, 76; specialized stock groups, 77
New York Times, 52, 189
No-load mutual funds, 16, 71, 89, 151
NOW accounts, 41, 46–47; in personalized portfolios, 159, 160, 162, 169, 170, 178, 184
Numismatic dealers, 128
Nuveen Tax-Exempt Mutual Fund, 51

Odd lot investments, 78
Oil and gas exploration, 10, 26
"100 Highest Yields," 54
Open-ended funds, 85, 94
Options markets, 27, 138–42
OTC (Over the counter market), 75, 77
Ovest Securities, 82
"Out of the money" calls, 139–40, 142

Pace Securities, 82
Pacific Brokerage Services, 82
Pacific Coast Savings and Loan, 52
Packard, David, 26
Palladium, 123, 134
Parents, and tax savings, 121–22
Parker, Alexander, 83
Partnerships, 12–15
"Passbook" savings accounts, 3, 40. See also Banks, savings accounts in
Pass thru securities, 68–72, 185
PCs (Participation Certificates), 71–72
PE, 74
Penalties. See Withdrawal penalties
Pennsylvania, 177
Pension funds, 60, 66, 69
Pensions, 143, 153
Permanent life insurance, 18–19
Perot, H. Ross, 26
Personal Investor, 191
Platinum, 123, 130, 134
Precious metals, 29, 123–34; funds, 87; in personalized portfolio, 182–83
Preferred stock, 79–80; convertible, 135–36
Prefunded bonds, 105
Premiums, in options, 139–42
Price/earnings ratio (PE), 74
Prices: corporate bonds, 55, 61–62; covered options, 138–42; gold and silver, 124, 132; platinum, 134; tax-exempts, 100; Treasury bonds, 56–57
Prospectuses, 13, 62–64, 95
Puerto Rico, 103, 110
Put provisions, 62, 106
Put tax-exempt bonds, 102, 106–107, 187
Puts, 138–40

Quick and Reilly, 83

Ratings: corporate bonds, 59–60, 63; junk bonds, 60; tax-exempts, 101–102
Real estate, 6, 10, 119
"Real" interest, 22–23, 124, 145
Registered tax-exempt bonds, 97
Research and information, on securities, 12–13, 16, 29–31, 137–38, 189–92
Retirement investments, 143–53; and permanent life insurance, 18–19; zero coupon bonds and, 66. See also Investment strategies, and retirement
Revenue tax-exempt bonds, 100–102, 105
RHM Convertible Survey, 138
Risk, 7–8; convertibles, 137; corporate bonds, 60–61, 63; and diversification,

26–27; Government bonds, 57; mutual funds, 84–89, 109; options, 140–41; tax-exempts, 102; and tax shelters, 10
Rockefeller, John D., 25
"Round-trip" sale, 4, 104–105, 128–29
Rowe Price funds, 49, 51, 65, 149

SAFECO Funds, 65, 150
Sales charges, 16, 85, 114, 130
Savings, 18–22
Savings accounts. See Banks, savings accounts in; IRAs
Savings and loan associations, 39–40, 147, 150
Schwab One, 84
Scudder Funds, 49, 51, 150
Securities and Exchange Commission, 43
Self-employed investment strategy, 170–71
Self-employed retirement accounts, 151–53, 152 n
Serial tax-exempt bonds, 97
Series EE bonds, 116
Share discount brokers, 81–82
Share/Value discount brokers, 83
Shearson/American Express, 129
Short-term bank CDs, 44–47, 55, 148; in personalized portfolio, 161
Short-term government securities. See T-bills
Silver, 123, 130, 132–34
Simple interest, 20
Small Business Administration, 58
South Africa, 123, 126, 134; gold stocks, 129, 131; Krugerrand, 126–28
Soviet Union, 123, 134
Specialized mutual funds, 87, 92–93, 95
Split-rate CDs, 45
Standard and Poor's credit ratings, 59, 101
Standard and Poor's 500, 76–77, 89
State and local governments: sales tax on gold coins, 125–26; taxes on income, 44, 47, 57, 59, 116; tax-exempt bonds, 96–103, 105, 107; zero coupon bonds, 66–68
"Statement" savings accounts, 40
Steinroe Bond Fund, 65
Sterling, 132
Stern, Phillip, 8
Stock exchanges, 75–78, 85
Strike price, 138–42
Sunshine Mining, 133
Sylvia Porter's Personal Finance Magazine, 191
Syndicated limited partnerships. See Limited partnerships

Tax brackets, 96–97, 102–103, 117; and deferred variable annuity, 165; and IRA withdrawals, 144, 147; and split-rate CDs, 45; tables, 98–99; and trusts and gifts, 117–118, 120–22
Tax credits, 8–9, 9 n

Tax deductions: family income transfers and, 118; and IRAs, 144–45; and limited partnerships, 14–15; mortgage interest and, 25; bond swaps and, 103–104 See also Tax shelters

Tax deferrals, 9–11, 13, 19, 117; annuities, 112–115, 165.
See also IRAs; Keogh retirements

Tax-exempt bond funds, 108–112, 177

Tax-exempt bonds, 8–9, 11, 16, 22, 75, 117; basic information, 96–100; money market funds, 50–51, 163, 183, 187; ratings, 100–102; swapping of, 103; tax bracket tables, 98–99; types of, 104–112; zero coupon, 67–68, 107. See also Tax-exempt put bonds; Tax-exempt unit trusts

Tax-exempt put bonds, 106–107, 187

Tax-exempt unit trusts, 17, 106–108, 111–112, 177, 187

Tax laws, 9, 24–25; and income transfers, 118–22, 121 n

Tax shelters, 8–11, 17; limited partnerships, 13–15; mutual funds and IRAs, 149–50; preferred stock, 79

Tax swaps, 103–104

T-bills, 39, 43–44, 46, 65, 106; advantages, 47; buying of, 44, 53; money market investments, 48–49; and preservation of capital, 125

Term life insurance, 18–19

Texas, 44–45

Texas Instruments Student Business Analyst-35 pocket calculator, 21

Thrifts, 40–42, 44

TIGRs (Treasury Investment Growth Receipts), 67

Time-Life publications, 190

Treasury strips, 67

Trusts, 118–21

United Services Gold Shares, 129–30

United States, 123, 129; interest on CDs, 44; deregulation of interest ceilings, 40–42, 45–47; federal agency bonds, 57–59; gold coins, 126–28, 131; prefunded bonds, 105; securities laws, 7, 13; silver coins, 132–33; tax laws, 8–11, 117–22.

See also Congress; T-bills; U.S. Savings Bonds; U.S. Treasury bonds

U. S. Postal Service, 58

U. S. Savings Bonds, 115–117; in personalized portfolio, 175

U. S. Treasury bills. See T-bills

U. S. Treasury bonds, 21 n, 58–60, 69, 97, 105; listings, 56–57; price, 57, 61; zero coupon, 66–67

Unit trusts. See Bond unit trusts; Ginnie Maes, unit trusts; Tax-exempt unit trusts

Universal life insurance, 19

"University Trust 1," 120–21

Up markets, 86, 142

Value discount brokers, 81–82

Value Line funds, 65, 150

Value Line Investment Survey, 17, 31, 80, 192

Vanguard Group funds, 49, 65, 150

Vanguard GNMA Portfolio, 71

Vanguard High Yield Bond Portfolio, 61

Vanguard Insured Money Market Portfolio, 49

Variable annuities, 114–115; in personalized portfolio, 165

Variable rate CDs, 45

Variable rate mortgages, 25

Wall Street Discount, 82

Wall Street Journal, 10, 52, 95, 107, 189

Wang, An, 26

Western Gulf Savings and Loan, 52

Whole life insurance, 18

Wilson, Roger W., 15

Wisconsin, 44, 57

Withdrawal penalties: CDs, 45, 53; deferred annuities, 113–114, 165; IRAs, 146–48, 159, 171; Keoghs, 152–53; U. S. Savings Bonds, 117

World Bank, 58

Yield. See Interest rates

Yield to maturity, 57, 67–68

Zero coupon bonds, 45, 119; discussed, 65–68; tax-exempts, 105, 107